EFFING SIMPLE LEADERSHIP

How to Take Back Control and Make an Impact on Every Part of Your Life

BY
TONI VANSCHOYCK
& EFFING VISONARY POWERHOUSES

Copyright © 2021 by Toni Vanschoyck.

All rights reserved. No part of this publication may be reproduced, distributed, or transmitted in any form or by any means, including photocopying, recording, or other electronic or mechanical methods, without the prior written permission of the author, except in the case of brief quotations embodied in critical reviews and certain other non-commercial uses permitted by copyright law.

Ordering Information: Quantity sales. Special discounts are available on quantity purchases by corporations, associations, and others. Orders by U.S. trade bookstores and wholesalers.

www.DreamStartersPublishing.com

TONI VANSCHOYCK & EFFING VISIONARY
POWERHOUSES

Table of Contents

Introduction 4

Leadership – A Service 10

Leading with Heart 26

Gratitude – The Game Changer 42

Family 56

Faith 73

Leading Yourself 87

Courage 103

Integrity 116

Why 131

Finance 143

Mind and Vision 155

Introduction

The world is a crowded place. With billions of lives waking up every single day, it is fascinating to realize how each of these lives shares some common goals, despite all the differences that may exist. Underneath the skin, we are all the same. We all have wants, needs, and desires. We all breathe the same air and eat the same food, and we even might dream the same dreams. If that is the case, why is it that only a handful of these billions go on and lead happier, successful, joyous lives while others continue to find themselves in a vicious cycle of "work, eat, sleep, and repeat?" Surely, there must be something that these few are doing something differently, or perhaps, they are the "chosen ones," if you believe in that kind of stuff.

While most of us continue to dream big, but say no when the opportunity is presented, only a select few step forward, step up and choose to lead the way. They are the people who realize that leadership isn't something that is conjured up by a group of people who possess special skills or knowledge and it actually takes work. They grasp the concept of leadership and lead as an example for others because they chose to and it is speaking to their heart and soul.

TONI VANSCHOYCK & EFFING VISIONARY POWERHOUSES

To many, this may come as a bit of a surprise, but I assure you that it is true. *Effing Simple Leadership* is not just another book that I decided to write. For years, I have seen many people struggling with their lives, thinking they will never be able to do the kind of things they dreamt of, and the way they go about their business, they just might be right. However, through this book, I intend to change that.

If you have read the last two books of mine, you know that I am not here to talk about things that are completely irrelevant or that miss the point. Just like the last two books, which have been straight to the point, no bullshit, this book will follow the same approach.

Throughout this book, you will come across real-life lessons and not just the ones that I experienced. This book is made possible through the collaboration of inspiring leaders and visionaries who agreed to share their stories with the readers, allowing everyone to learn from their perspective. These are people that moved my world and they will move yours.

While there are many books out there, written by truly inspirational people, they tend to talk from the perspective of the writer alone. Although there is still something for everyone to learn it isn't always relatable. It is human nature that we tend to learn from things that we can connect with and relate to. By introducing a multitude of perspectives, each of these life lessons will help us learn all about what leadership is, and how one can go on to become a top leader.

You can be a 21-year-old student, a 45-year-old professional, a 35-year-old housewife, a 70 something grandparent, or anyone else for that matter, and you will still find something worthwhile in this book. The objective isn't to repeat what is already available on the internet, but to explore, with rich examples, tips, and recommendations that will truly help you propel your career, your success, and ultimately, your life towards your goals.

Before we do move ahead, there is something that needs to be clarified right away. So many people, when presented with the term 'leadership,' instantly assume that we are talking business. Leadership isn't just limited to a business environment; it exists in virtually EVERY aspect of life. You can be a great leader to your family, guide them accordingly, and ensure they succeed in life. You can be a great leader as a mentor, teach those who are struggling to move forward and achieve their success. Furthermore, you can be a true leader and lead a group of people that share the same interests or goals. To do any of these, to be able to help anyone else and lead, you need leadership skills, and above all, you need to decide to be a leader right now!

If you are someone who is still doubtful of how you could go on to become a leader in life and acquire the almighty skill of leadership, stop right here! Stop whatever it is that you are doing, close your eyes, and tell yourself out loud:

"I choose to be a leader in life. I will lead on every front. I will not cave into the challenges, and I will face them head-on!"

Don't worry, you will learn just why I asked you to do so. You might be surprised to know that simplicity can help you excel at a phenomenal rate. It's all about letting yourself know that you have a choice, and then choosing to be a leader for the rest of your life.

Many of the contributors in this book will highlight how they had a completely different life back then, and how each of them were on a divine path of leadership. Their stories are inspiring, and even that is an understatement. They have managed to change their lives, and everything about them and their surroundings to fall in line with their vision and goals. They broke away the shackles, despite having a vast number of challenges before them, and they continued to persevere. Today, each of these women, myself included, enjoys a life that they can truly cherish. They are no longer bound by any restrictions, whether physical, emotional, social or any other form. They get to choose what they want to do, and they go out to do exactly that.

You will also learn 15 important traits that contribute, and ultimately make an individual a leader. These key traits are:

- Understanding your 'why'
- Learning to lead yourself – remember; change starts with you!
- Family
- Faith
- Gratitude
- Finance
- Fitness
- Understanding how your brain is wired
- Friends
- Your integrity
- Courage
- Service
- Leading with your heart
- Your vision
- Daily activities

With so much to learn and so little time, let's not eff around and dive straight into it!

"Success isn't how much money one makes, or how significant of a business they end up creating, but it is the freedom to live and lead in life that truly defines success."

Jessica Schone is a wife and mom to 4 kids. She was a salon owner and hair stylist 16 years. Monat has allowed her to now work her business full time from home while raising her kids and making an impact locally and globally through gratitude.

Chapter 1

Leadership – A Service

By Jessica Schone

Life, in itself, is one of the rare things that no one can predict. Some go on to live for as long as a century, while most perish well before hitting the 70 marks. It is a natural process, one that we can never come to control. Worrying too much about how your life will end is, therefore, fruitless. It is inevitable, and you can invest as much money as you like, but you will still not be able to buy a second more time.

However, with a bit of a change in perspective, you end up gaining a completely new meaning to life. Instead of worrying about the inevitable, and what might happen when

LEADERSHIP – A SERVICE

that time comes, how about the focus on how much you would have achieved by leading your life successfully when that day comes? Almost immediately, things change. Now, there is room for possibilities, opportunities, and probabilities. The funny thing is, all this room was always there, waiting for you to just take the first step towards it. It took nothing more than the smallest of efforts, and a change of perspective to figure out a world full of possibilities that lies between then and now.

What you make with that time is life itself. You can either let things 'happen' and become a passenger, who is aimlessly taken around with zero direction, or you can swap seats and be the driver yourself and drive towards where you truly wish to go. The choice has always been yours!

Leadership isn't something that a small number of people are born with. Every child that breathes their first lung-full of oxygen brings with them a quality of leadership. As the child grows, many factors surrounding that child either promote this quality or help suppress it. It is a quality that can shine bright, or hide within us somewhere. It can never perish.

Leadership is a choice, and Jessica Schone is the embodiment of that. She has gone on to teach many students what it takes to be a leader, and how leadership is as simple as choice.

Jessica is a wife and a proud mother of 4 kids. For a good part of her life, she has been an owner of a salon and has worked as a hairstylist for 16 years. One would say that she is leading a joyous and successful life. Truth be told, it wasn't always like that. Had she not chosen to find the will within her to put the foot down and decide enough was enough, things would have been very different.

There is no denying that change is a universal constant. It happens even if the world is not prepared for it. This is often why people hate change or are far too afraid of what change may bring for them later on. For Jessica, it wasn't a hard choice at all. To be the best person for her family, to be a leader, and to be a role model for her children, she chose to seek out change. It wasn't easy, but she endured everything, faced every challenge that came in her way, and today, the world is looking forward to learning from her.

While she credits much of her achievement, and how she went on to develop leadership, to her mentors, it is her own will, perseverance and commitment that ensured her success. Riding above all of that was her consistency, which quite a few people tend to undermine and overlook. It is through consistency that you develop momentum, and it is that momentum that pushes you forward.

"If more people would realize that leadership is a choice, and not just something that magically appears, I think that more people would choose to do it."

LEADERSHIP – A SERVICE

Leadership is both a choice and a commitment. Considering that Jessica operates within the Arts industry, she goes on to talk about how leaders possess a leadership mindset. She quotes Luke 16:10, from the Bible:

"Whoever can be trusted with very little can also be trusted with much, and whoever is dishonest with very little will also be dishonest with much"

Jessica teaches her students that if they, as individuals, aim to be a leader in a business, just walk the walk and think and act like someone who is at the very top of whatever business they are in. Look at how they work, how they behave, what they do, and what they tend to avoid. By being in the shoes of these top ladder leaders, one can get a solid idea of what changes they must bring within themselves. Remember, leadership is a choice, and that means that you already have everything you need to be a leader. All you need is to identify what skills you need to work on and which ones you should drop. As John Maxwell says focus on your strengths and outsource your weaknesses.

Jessica isn't a superhuman being either. She too went through the same trials in life that most of us are busy complaining about every single day. The difference, however, is simple; she chose not to let her hardships control her life.

She did not settle to be defined as "just another person" and she certainly did not like the idea of just being an existence.

She decided to find the time to reflect upon her life, figure out what was going wrong, and then take the steps that needed to be taken. Opportunity doesn't come to you; you go create an opportunity for yourself. Those who wait, unsurprisingly, continue to wait and that can turn into a lifetime. She had already taken the first step by preparing herself to make changes. I assure you, making life changes is one of the hardest challenges you can face, and that is why a lot of people tend to back out or give up far too early. It is only after taking this bold first step that you can truly realize a bigger, better and more meaningful life ahead.

Jessica went on to be part of a business endeavor, and that is where she found guidance, a sense of fulfillment, achievement and motivation. Meeting like-minded people, she realized that she wasn't the only one who was struggling and that everyone within the room shared the same common goals and objectives. She found herself a chance to renew everything, set the terms right, and find leadership. Since then, Jessica has been a beacon of light, a ray of hope for all those who continue to struggle in life. Mastering the skills, she now intends to share her knowledge, experiences, and help everyone lead better lives as well, ones where they are in control.

Leading the Way

Jessica explains that it isn't hard to be a leader, but that does not mean that it is easy either. As a leader, it is up to you to guide the people who are seeking your guidance and leadership to move forward. For some people, they will never be able to see anything beyond what you show them, and that isn't a matter of choice either. As a leader, you are the one with the bigger picture in mind, a bird's eye view of the entire situation. Choosing what path must be followed is up to you. Once you know what needs to be done, your leadership skills will ensure that others go on to do just that. In simpler terms, they cannot see what you can, and what you choose to show them, they will believe in that!

She goes on to talk about how important it is to think and act like you have made it to the top, as opposed to hoping that you will one day make it. The ideology is simple; action equals results. Hoping simply doesn't cut it.

When you start working your business like a leader who is successful and at the top of the game, you will automatically start gaining the trust of those around you. This isn't just limited to business either. You can use the same approach in any aspect of life, and end up seeing the same results.

By presenting yourself as a weak link, someone who is miserable struggling, you will never be able to instill a sense of confidence in those you choose to interact with. Just put yourself in the same situation and imagine someone approaching you, telling you how difficult of a life they are living and how everything seems hopeless. How would you feel? Of course, you may empathize, but you wouldn't exactly be confident about trusting them.

If you truly wish to be a leader, the first rule is to stop being miserable and start actively being grateful for everything you have right now in this very moment. No one is willing to follow a self-proclaimed leader who offers nothing but negativity and discouragement.

Jessica owned a salon for 8 years, and she knew everything that goes into making a salon successful. She had experienced, learned and understood everything, from the very top to the bottom. Later on, she started in another business. Needless to say, she was expecting this to be completely different, structurally speaking, but she was surprised to learn that it was almost identical. This simply shows that business, no matter whatever niche it may be targeting, is structurally uniform. This also proves that people who often worry far too much about a business being something new, and something that they may not be able to comprehend, do so in vain.

As a business owner, the first rule is to commit to leadership. It may be a choice, but remember that it is also a full-time commitment. Whatever your business may be,

LEADERSHIP – A SERVICE

however it may be performing, you must show up to work every single day, with no room for excuses. As a leader, it is you who gets to set the benchmark for quality, productivity and everything business-related. You must have the 'yes' mindset, and share that positivity. Reflect that your business means something. It is only after you gain this mindset that people turn back to say yes to you as well.

People often waste their time worrying far too much about things that aren't in play yet, and how the unknown will go on to affect them, and to Jessica it's nothing but a trap. Those caught within this trap are never able to move ahead in life, let alone succeed. As a leader, it is our job to overlook these traps and be the leader for others. As leaders, people will come to you for solutions, and you must lead them to a solution. Be the one to tell them that you will solve the problem together and allow them to gain your trust. Get the job done, and you end up creating a loyal customer, who will keep coming back to you in the future because you have created that bond.

A leader always knows what needs to be done, and is not afraid to take the necessary action and 90% of the time you know the answer--follow your intuition. It is there for a reason. Let the overthink and perfection go and just take that step forward it is that effing simple. Many successful leaders in life keep everything simple, and that is where people often go wrong. There is no reason to complicate things in business or life in general. You lead, they follow, you offer a solution, and they take it – end of story!

Back when Jessica was still operating a salon, she took initiative and adopted the 'yes' mindset by taking on the challenge of launching her new business. Her radiating confidence alone attracted others to come on board partner with her. She brought in customer after customer, purely because of her winning mindset.

People are drawn not by the perks that they are offered, but by the leadership skills at display that instill a sense of confidence in them. From there, it's all about consistency and how committed you remain to your vision. Your commitment to your customers, and those seeking solutions and leadership, now becomes service.

It takes time to build up trust, to gain the level of confidence you need to make anything work for you but you only gain that by practicing, practicing again and practicing more which leads to confidence. Through your confidence, you reassure your loved ones, customers, and clients that you know what you are doing. This is exactly the reason why you often see Elon Musk talking about his visions and goals, followed by investors from all around the world pouring in for him. It is his confidence talking because everyone knows, "He knows what he is talking about!"

Jessica was able to do all of that, and she was able to win the trust of people who wanted to work with her, and

LEADERSHIP – A SERVICE

people who wanted to do business with her, and that too before she even began. It shows that building trust has virtually nothing to do with the business you are involved in, but it is all about how you use your leadership skills and reflect confidence. What Jessica was doing can best be defined as "Service Equity."

Let's define what that is. It is simply putting others first and helping them to win. How can I serve you and how can I help you win? Jessica is already doing a fabulous job at teaching just that. What people fail to realize is that this is a life-long commitment to being a leader, earning the trust of those whom you may work with, or whom you may conduct business with, will eventually grow into something truly substantial, and it is that Service Equity that can then go on to create magic.

Choosing Leadership

Leadership is not something a people are born with but a choice for everyone, it all boils down to one simple question; will you make the choice? Are you slightly intimidated?

The idea of bringing about this massive change in life is intimidating at times, and it is completely natural to feel that way. What is not natural is the fact that we allow that fear to consume us, barring us from making a move that we truly want to. More than half of people will back off immediately.

From that remainder, not even a quarter will muster up the courage to say "Yes! I am ready for the change!"

The good news, which should bring some comfort to us, is that we can all do it. If you do not believe me, take Jessica's word for it. She has been there, and she has done it, and come through all the way just to let you know that you can do it too.

Jessica perfectly explains how easy it is to make this choice. She goes on to quote a verse from Isaiah of the Bible (41:10):

"Fear not, for I am with you; be not dismayed, for I am your God; I will strengthen you, I will help you, I will uphold you with my righteous right hand."

She was significantly confident because she knew what she was walking into, and presenting to possible clients. Although at times she was fearful she persevered. And when you practice something enough it equates to confidence. Her confidence radiated motivation and reassurance to others, allowing them to make a sound decision about their lives that they may have never made otherwise. When you practice the behaviors and lead by example it cascades down to your business, employees, family and your entire circle. This was her service equity in action, influencing and persuading others

LEADERSHIP – A SERVICE

to follow her lead, not because they had no other alternative, but because they knew Jessica, and they trusted her.

Of course, not everyone is on board right away. Some questioned the idea of changing their ways or following her into an unknown. It is only natural that one would find both support and resistance at the same time, and it is nothing to feel guilty about.

For her husband was among the first ones who did not find himself comfortable with the idea of jumping into in the network marketing industry, and you can't blame him either. Jessica knew that not everyone would understand and see the vision right away. There will always be naysayers who will either tell you that you are wrong or continue to point out flaws in whatever it is that you are doing. Instead of paying attention to the naysayers, work on your leadership, your actions, and your income-producing activities towards your objectives because that is time better spent.

Every business professional, entrepreneur, and individual must understand that leadership isn't just about winning customers trust or getting to the next level and record sales figures. It's more than that. Leadership is, in the simplest form, about helping others.

She realized that her passion to create an environment where other employees would want to work was real and that she had the qualities and the capabilities to make that happen. This is exactly why she quit her job and decided to open her own business instead. Her leadership abilities saw things through and she was able to do exactly what she had sought out to do in the first place and ran a very lucrative salon and wedding hair business.

With her network marketing business, she emphasized that she wanted to grow the right team that shared her passion to work and lead as an example with gratitude. Make no mistake, it is a huge responsibility on your shoulders because people tend to join based on what they see in you. You've earned their trust Jessica further explains that being in a people business, there are three aspects to service.

1. The team itself. Everyone on your team is saying yes to you to work with you, and be led by you.

It doesn't matter if the team comprises a single person, or one hundred which essentially is to look over the entire operation and ensure everyone onboard is being taken care of. Once you can take care of a single person, it will go on to prepare you to do the same for many others as well and it will become a domino effect.

2. Customers. It is of utmost importance to us, as individuals and business owners, that we connect with the customer and "plug them in," so that they do not feel lost (products, discounts, how to set up their

account, etc.). Some customers may have a good idea of what they want, or what they can expect from you, but many would be clueless. That is where we need our leadership skills to guide them accordingly. She ensures that her customers know exactly how to use the products/services they end up purchasing because that further helps in promoting confidence and business overall. It also ensures that they do not miss out on the products that are the best for them.

3. YOU, as a person and a leader. Many tend to work on the first two points, but they often overlook the importance of the third, and that is a major mistake. To put it simply, if you can't take care of yourself, you can't expect yourself to be in any condition to take care of others. If you are well, fully committed and driven, only then can you help your customers and lead your team. Take some time out to ensure you invest something in yourself, whether it is to take a break, rejuvenate, groom well, dress well, or anything along those lines. By doing so, you not only promote your personality, but you set a benchmark for others to automatically follow and adopt.

Helping Others Achieve Freedom

Jessica explains that her choice to become a leader and to be able to lead the way in which she does, all comes down to how all of that helps others achieve what they desire in life. She says "I believe that I am helping people accomplish something that allows them to have time freedom." It allows them to be able to successfully run a business that is not always how the world paints it. It is something that is different and allows flexibility and freedom. Above all, it provides them with the potential to earn as much as they desire."

As a leader, her priorities are to ensure that those who said yes to her, are reaching their goals, and she does that by being an effective leader. It sometimes is a heavy responsibility, but it is one that holds endless rewards.

It isn't before your leadership goes on to help someone succeed in their life that you truly feel accomplished. Witnessing them succeed, and knowing that you got to be their mentor and most important - guide them. This is a feeling that cannot be replicated by any other achievement in life. Jessica is no stranger to such a feeling.

Nick, her husband, had an aunt who was living several states away. She was going through a rough patch. She was running a home day-care, and although she loved the kids she watched, she would always be worn out and a slave to

LEADERSHIP – A SERVICE

the demand of the work. On top of that, she had a family of her own to look after. During this time, Jessica spoke to her about switching businesses and taking a leap, to which she responded with every single excuse in the book. She would say ". How can you expect me to run a business that revolves around something I have no idea about?"

It didn't take long before Jessica was able to convince her to stop worrying so much and start taking the action. Soon afterwards, she was able to close her day-care business. She has been doing the business full time, and her life has changed completely.

Success isn't how much money one makes, or how significant of a business they end up creating, but it is the freedom to live and lead in life that truly defines success. You may own a billion-dollar company, but if you cannot call the shots, lead a life that fulfils you, and gives you peace of mind that all your hard work is rewarded justly, you aren't successful at all. The same mindset can be applied to any business. Consider this as a "one-size-fits-all" kind of a deal. If you can find the courage within you to push yourself forward, bring out the best version within you, and be confident about your choice, you are bound to taste success. Your journey will continue to inspire and motivate others around you, even if you do not notice that happening yet.

Chapter 2

Leading with Heart

By Jessica Schone

If you are someone who knows the kind of a person Jessica is, you would know that she would always emphasize how leadership is a choice, and I cannot see any reason why shouldn't do so. I have met more people in my life than I can count, and a vast majority of them were simply unaware of how leadership is a choice. Although I could find ways to show them that they were wrong, nothing can compare to the confidence that Jessica has when she teaches her students all about leadership.

Jessica is a woman of faith, meaning that she puts her heart in whatever she believes in. Our hearts only know what they like and what they don't, and everything in the middle is where our brain kicks in. If you were to bypass your brain for a moment there and let your heart do the talking, decisions would become a lot easier to make. You would either make an effort to become a leader or you wouldn't.

    Jessica chose to be a leader in every business that she walked into. She would always listen to her heart and lead with it. If it moved, she would do the same. If her heart didn't feel right about something, she would shut those doors without any second thoughts. This often meant that she took monumental risks, the kind of which would leave most of us biting our nails out, and yet, she was as calm as ever. She shows that choosing something that involves risk will always be something that rewards the most, and it is true.

    Throughout our academic years, we have been taught how high-risk decisions will yield high returns, but when an opportunity presents itself to us, we tend to look at the possible downfall that may or may not happen. We allow ourselves to be consumed by the fear of losing everything. She does the complete opposite. She takes the risk first, following her heart, and is determined to help those who find themselves stuck, without ever worrying about the possibility of things going south. While her risk-taking ability is commendable, it is her sheer faith that goes on to pretty much guarantee her success. Whether it is her faith rewarding her or because of the dedication and commitment she brings to the table, the bottom line is that leading from the heart works.

"Let us not become weary in doing good, for at the proper time we will reap a harvest if we do not give up."

Galatians 6:9

Jessica fuses both her faith and her wisdom to bring forth a completely new perspective. It is her faith, her confidence, knowledge and skills that allow her to do the kind of things she does. She further says:

"To be diligent, choose to lead despite how you feel, commit to yourself, and those who trust you, and say yes to you, and make sure you pay attention to your heart."

As a leader, it is understood that others will always continue to look up to you, hoping to seek out some wisdom, some guidance, and it is then that where your heart will start working, telling you what you must do and what you shouldn't.

A lot of people tend to find themselves questioning everything far more than needed and wastes time and reflects a lack of confidence. She not only knows what she is doing, but she finds answers in seemingly impossible situations. I've been a mentor to Jess for five years and this is one of the reasons why people continue to place their trust in her, allowing her to be the leader they choose to follow. People are attracted to energy, that spark that is present and overwhelming. Take that out of the equation, and you instantly lose your leadership skills, the trust of the customers and clients, and the life of the business.

Drifting Away? It's Natural!

There will come a time where you might start questioning "Why am I doing this?" or "Do I still have what it takes to be successful in life?" She explains quite beautifully,

"This is a very natural feeling. Part of the reason why that happens is the fact that everything takes time to take shape and present itself to you. Not everyone is patient in life, and it is very easy for people to find themselves feeling lost, stagnant or losing the energy and the spark that kept them moving forward every day."

Let's use an example. My imaginary friend Brad starts going to the gym regularly because he wants to bulk up and gain muscle. He does everything by the book, makes sure he's getting his proteins and aminos and makes sure he is burning enough calories between weight exercises and cardio. The first few months, you can see a difference in his physique, and after a few months of improvement, he starts to plateau. This is because this person has already gone through the first initial transformational phases, which were relatively easy, but anything ahead of this point takes even more consistency and dedication. It's the same with your team's success in business. Your team/business' numbers are climbing and it's exciting! Then, you get comfortable and wonder why they've hit a plateau. Constant growth demands consistency and commitment. The same principle applies to every single area of life. If you find yourself and your heart stuck at a point in time, know that you need to keep the momentum going. Once you get over that "stuckedness," the numbers will climb again because you continued to pour in the efforts despite the challenges that came before you.

    We are human beings, and as Jessica puts it, *"We don't always feel motivated, happy, energetic, or even feel like we are making any difference. That is where your heart can play a vital role. That is where your faith and following your heart can help you maintain a steady course in life."*
It helps you from deviating from what you are doing and allows you to continue to believe that good will prevail in the end.

> "My whole life, being involved in the business that I've been involved in, whenever I was feeling like that, I had gone to prayer. A door would always open, literally. It would always be up to me to make a choice and walk through the door."

LEADING WITH HEART

This is so true. If you are someone who believes that they are lost, resort to prayer, listen to your heart, and you will always find a passageway that helps you move forward. Yes, you may stumble across numerous obstacles, but unless you do not choose to move forward, you aren't moving at all, and that is a true failure.

At a company convention, about 2 years ago, Jessica had the opportunity to speak publicly which made her feel conflicted. She was supposed to speak about Building Your Business but felt so heavy on her heart to use this opportunity to make a difference. Towards the end of her speech, she shared the opportunity with 8,000 people, that they could help her raise funds to build a compassion center in Columbia, on behalf of the owners of the company (They're from Venezuela), as a way to thank them for all they have done. She knew that this was so meaningful, yet she was so scared. She remembers her mouth was completely dry and that she was sweating. Her mind was bombarded with questions because she wasn't too sure if they would be proud of what she was doing and would want to support this mission. However, being the kind of person Jessica is, she led with her heart. What was supposed to be an opportunity to raise funds for a single compassion center, was so successful that she ended up raising money for FOUR centers.

She is filled with utter joy when thinking back on this moment, knowing that she not only proposed an idea that was instantly supported but it helped so many South & Central American families Moments like these reassure her that leading with her heart, even if it wasn't for herself, can create some of the most inspiring outcomes.

What Jessica was able to do still leaves me at a loss. Through the power of one, she was able to raise well over $340,000 in just 3 months. It was the whole community, but it was h who led that community into making this possible. So many people stepped up and said "Yes, I will help." and it was only because Jessica believed in what her heart was leading her to do.

She further explains that people often ignore what their hearts have to say, and that is a massive mistake. The heart is essentially the subconsciousness speaking and for to Jessica, God speaking. It's proven that the subconscious mind can be considerably more powerful because it knows what you are truly capable of. While the conscious mind dwindles on the 'pros' and 'cons' of a situation, challenge, or opportunity, it's the heart that says "Yes" or "No," without the extra work of going into the details. It is the biggest motivator for anyone, and for Jessica, it is her heart that pushes her to not only change her life and people she loves when she enters Network Marketing, but also many that she doesn't even know.

Heart Over Mind

The majority of people prioritize their thoughts and what they mean. They believe that their mind is the most powerful organ, that allows them to make "smart" decisions, safe decisions, and better decisions. Jessica disagrees. By following what her heart has told her by paying attention to her heart's desires, she was able to establish an even bigger Gratitude movement through her business.

It started with her heart telling her to stop with her job in a salon and start her own business as a salon owner. Had she not taken that step, and not become a leader for herself and employees, she probably would have stayed in a job where she was told what hours to work and what weekends she could take off for her kids' sports events. She would be missing out on the important moments in life, have restricted financial freedom, and wouldn't be working for herself. As soon as she began her own salon business, and later her network marketing business, she was back in the driving seat, controlling her and her family's future.

Jessica says that this has helped her not only improve herself as a person and an individual, but it helped her grow deeper and more meaningful relationships with her family members, gain more business success than she thought possible, and an infinite number of friendships that accept her just as she is.

People who discredit their heart end up o missing out on the joys in life. They are voluntarily surrendering their freedom. If that isn't enough, they are then sacrificing their dreams. Pursuing something that your heart tells you that you need automatically lands you in a driver's seat position and helps create the best version of yourself every single day. You know that you are doing something you love, something that your heart wants, and you will leave no stone unturned. Take that away, and you are essentially doing something, because you "have to" do so.

"We all have our unique stories and the things we have walked through. It was an overcoming moment for me as well. It goes back to childhood. The things that were taught to you, things that surrounded you, and the fact that most of them weren't even your choice. By the time a person becomes an adult, they develop a belief that they cannot control most of the things in life, and that they have to make do with what they have."

When people's eyes are opened, it's a "Whoa!" moment. When they realize that the world has a lot more to offer than what they were led to believe, things start to change. As kids, we would normally hear our parents telling us what we should do because "that's where the "real," money lies." What about where our hearts lie? What about our passion? What if a person doesn't want to become a doctor, a lawyer, an engineer or a mechanic? Does this mean that they

LEADING WITH HEART

simply have no choice over their life and that they were born to follow? Wrong!

It is through acceptance of mediocrity and lack of inclination that adults decide not to follow their passion, and stay at their job because "the money is good." Money isn't the answer for everything. Even the legendary Hollywood actor Jim Carrey says:

"I think everybody should get rich and famous and do everything they ever dreamed of so they can see that it's not the answer."

If money isn't the answer, why is society so hell-bent on telling us otherwise? It's because no one wants to be the odd one out that doesn't have a boss telling them what to do. Following their passion makes them a risk-taker. Society doesn't love those. There are too many naysayers out there, and unfortunately, some of them emerge from one's own family, friend circle, and even peer group.

Your mind and your heart can be best friends if you connect the two.

Leadership is about taking charge. It's having the ability to listen to your heart and being honest. It's about being able to influence others to see the path to success. It is a commitment, and it comes with responsibility as well. This is why a lot of people back away from becoming great leaders because they are "meant to follow" or are "comfortable following someone's lead." Some often take the back seat and let others take the lead deliberately, just to see what will happen - being a follower is not leadership behavior. The only one at a loss here is the one who failed to move ahead on time.

Can You Be a Leader?

Jessica says, "everyone is and can be a leader, you simply have to choose to recognize it and move with it." Jessica walks the walk. To be a leader, you do not have to be in a specific business, nor hold a specific set of skills or even any kind of specialized knowledge. It is a choice that you can make right here, right now. People don't know when they need to make this choice, though. Some leaders are forced to make this choice. Whether it is because of the straining situation they find themselves in, or they feel they are lacking purpose, losing their goals and not going anywhere. To some, things must get extremely tough before they decide enough is enough. It takes someone true to themselves to be able make such a difficult decision.

Jessica has seen this happen a million times and has guided those people to become leaders. By teaching them how to listen to their heart and pursue that, she has helped transform people into leaders they didn't even know they were.

LEADING WITH HEART

People can bring all the energy to the table, all the commitment and hard work, but without passion, they are only a shell – a mere existence in a physical form. It is our heart that makes us human, allows us to dream, helps us know what feels right and what doesn't, even if our mind is screaming the other way around. While our mind defines how intelligent we may be, it is our disposition and compassion that gives us a personality that is unique to us, that defines us as who we are.

Life is full of rollercoaster rides. Something may come up that you never thought you would want to pursue, or something you're not looking forward to. For Jessica, alignment is key. Because she is a woman of faith, if the word of God and her heart align, it's a go! There is not a second that she would waste, and she would make the decision instantly. She explains that God wouldn't just put something in her path for no fathomable reason. If it comes in her way, it is God's will. Whatever you believe in, opportunities come to you for a reason.

The process may be long, but, focus on the little things. If you can do these little things right, the big stuff will happen. Write your goals - break it down. By doing these smaller things right, you are still moving forward and growing closer to your ultimate goal.

The same applies to people. You start by taking care of the small stuff, helping one person at a time and bringing them into your circle. Before you know it, you could have a massive audience that is y waiting for you to share your wisdom, humor, experience and knowledge.

Todd Duncan often talks about the importance of micro-decisions. He believes that micro-decisions bring victory. The same micro-decisions can lead to failure as well. Confused?

Imagine yourself running a business where you are leading an excellent team. Every day, you wake up early, exercise, dress for success, plan out your day well before you reach the office, be the first one at work, ensure all tasks are done before the end of the day and help your employees with their challenges. All of these were micro-decisions you chose to make. No one forced you to do so, but you made these decisions because that's what gets things done. As a result, these micro-decisions will set a high-quality benchmark for your employees, ensuring that they arrive to work on time, work with as much energy as you, and deliver results.

On the other hand, let's say you have the same business, but own it. Now, you wake up every day and decide to hit the snooze button every time, just to get those golden minutes of sleep. You get out of bed exactly when you were supposed to arrive at the office. You dress casually, put on your sneakers, and arrive to work an hour late. Next, you go through the pile of work pending for you, but you have no idea what to prioritize, which is why you ask someone else to help

LEADING WITH HEART

you instead. Your business will start to lose its productivity. Employees will start arriving late, knowing that they won't get in trouble since you follow the same practices. If an issue arises, no one asks you for help because you don't even know what task to start with the dedication of the team will start to fade which will lead to o a decline/failure in business.

In both cases, you made micro-decisions, and in both situations, these micro-decisions went on to alter the outcome of the business future. See how this makes sense?

Of course, not everything in life comes bearing a label of "right" or "wrong," and that often leads people to making the wrong choices. Here are some questions that Jessica wants you to ask yourself when feeling conflicted.

- Will this be doing good?
- Does this align with my work?
- Is this going to help a lot of people?

You need to make sure that you have an answer for all three. Explore the outcome, as far as you know, the worst-case scenario is that you move on! Instead of calling it a failure, look at as another lesson you were able to learn or a new perspective seen. Failures are new perspectives... Read that again; failures are new perspectives. If you fail to pick up on the learning opportunity, and continue to do the same thing over and over, that is a failure.

She has changed many lives, and she will continue to do so in the future. I am so happy, and thankful that she expanded my view on what it means to truly lead with your heart and soul. If you are someone who constantly needs a source of motivation, guidance and direction, she is the one to seek out!

"If all your prayers were answered, would it change the world, or just yours?"

Kathy Yocum, is a business owner, entrepreneur and founder of 2 nonprofits in the State of Illinois, helping special needs. She is a dedicated Mother of 3 sons and grandmother of 5 and wife, living in Toledo, IL with her husband, Tim.

Chapter 3

Gratitude – The Game Changer

By Kathy Yocum

At the heart of leadership lies gratitude. It is gratitude that differentiates between people who tend to think they are leaders and those who truly are. Just imagine going through a day where you had to go through a lot of mishaps, face scenarios that didn't go as you might have wanted them to, and imagine how that would make you feel? Deflated, angry or ready to throw in the towel, right?

Based on these experiences, most of us would spend the rest of our days torturing ourselves, asking how any of this happened. While we are caught up doing that, we end up losing our temper, and we may, unintentionally, hurt those around us emotionally. It all sounds quite familiar, doesn't it? The fact is that leaders go through such phases too. After all, they are human beings. What differs between them and us is gratitude. Instead of focusing on what went wrong, how and why, they seek out positivity instead and learn from their mistakes. Instead of hurling abuse and blame on others, they reflect on the very same day and start counting the things that went right. It is nothing more than a new perspective, and the fact that these leaders appreciate everything that went well for them, expressing gratitude, and that helps them restore their morale, motivation, and energy. This also means that they will go home, and continue to enjoy quality time with their family members.

Outweighing the Good?

Once, I came across a story, and it proved to me just how quick we are to focus on the negatives, and how easily we tend to overlook all that went well. It is about a professor. that entered a classroom full of students. He grabbed a whiteboard marker and started scribbling multiplication tables. Obviously, an easy equation to solve. It seemed odd enough, but the students continued to pay attention.

The professor went on to write the entire table, eventually ending it at "2 x 10 = 20." As soon as he turned, he noticed the students were giggling, and some even burst into laughter. He asked "What happened? Did I do something wrong there," to which one of the students pointed out that he had written, "2 x 7 = 13."

He turned around, looked at the error, and smiled. He then said:

"I am glad that you noticed that because that is exactly what I wanted to teach. I made an error, and every one of you took no time in focusing on that. However, did anyone appreciate all that was right before and after that error, or did that all meant nothing because I ended up doing something wrong?"

Naturally, the laughter and giggles faded away instantly. This struck a chord with everyone, and everyone immediately understood what the lesson was; gratitude!

The Iron-Lady, Kathy!

There are far too many things in life that we should be thankful for, and yet, we tend to overlook the importance of gratitude. I have met a lot of people, and there is no one quite like **Kathy Yocum**, who can explain and highlight the importance of gratitude, and the blessings it can bring to our lives.

GRATITUDE – THE GAME CHANGER

Kathy Yocum, for those who may not know, is a successful business owner, entrepreneur and the founder of two non-profit organizations within the state of Illinois, both of which go on to help people with special needs. Besides being a figure of authority, success and gratitude, she is a dedicated mother of three sons, a grandmother of five, and a loving wife. She currently resides in Toledo, IL, along with her husband, Tim.

If anyone wants to experience gratitude, Kathy is the person. To her, gratitude simply means to put others above herself, make their lives simpler, all in the name of love. This isn't something that just occurred to her instantly. It was a long process, but one that came to fruition, and gave her the energy, positivity and determination to pursue what she wanted.

In Pursuit of Happiness

Kathy has what many would say a 'tear-jerking" story Even before she could move into adulthood, she found herself pregnant at the age of 16. All her dreams and ambitions were instantly brought to a shuddering halt. At that time, she was County Fair queen, an honor that most can only dream of having. When the time came to crown the new queen, she hid that fact she was 4 months pregnant, only her mother knew. She always felt like she had an unfinished life within the walls of her county. This is what led her to always try and find something that would allow her to fulfil her unfinished dream.

At the age of 58, she decided to step up and volunteer at the county fairgrounds. What followed was the opportunity to meet a lot of like-minded people, volunteers, and the opportunity to work on the tasks assigned to her. This is where opportunity came knocking. Volunteering became an outlet for Kathy to help because that's what she loved and still does today. It also a way for her to try to fulfil her dream, her life that could have been. Before she knew it, she was sitting at the center stage in Houston, Texas of her company's convention She distinctively remembers the writing across the main screen that read:

"If all your prayers were answered, would it change the world, or just yours?"

That, right there, was the bam-in-your-face moment that Kathy had been waiting for all this time. That, right there, was the answer to the questions that stormed her mind. She had been right all along, but she just didn't know it. She then went on to listen to the Director of Gratitude for the company, who asked everyone to go back to their own community and figure out how to help. This became a gratitude movement for Kathy It was further explained, "It's your time to bring something back to your community." There was no second-guessing what had just happened, or what was being asked of her. She knew in her mind, "That's exactly what I want to do." But what?

The Birth of a Dream

Sometimes, these revelations can take ages, but it is because of her constant and consistent efforts that she's poured in over the years and God led her right into her current business. Yes, she had no idea what she was doing there, but the big reveal instantly struck a chord with her, resonated with her on a level she did not know, and everything started to make sense. She wasn't there to sell products; she was there because the heavens wanted her to finish her dream.

When she got home, it was February of 2017, she did a searched and found an ad about some autistic equipment that would help those suffering with autism. She was involved with the YMCA and her boss wanted her to come up with a plan to help the autistic community. While they didn't use her plans, it gave her the confidence and the knowledge that things might work, and she of to communicate the Director of Gratitude, if accepted, would help a significant number of families. This was to specifically help people suffering from Autism. To her surprise, that single paragraph that she wrote was accepted immediately. She was accepted as the very first gratitude movement ambassador!

Prior to this, Kathy had no idea what autism meant, and she didn't shy away from admitting that. She had to rely on an internet search to provide her with the information. During her research, she was speaking to a local librarian about it, and that woman offered to help. Kathy received further information about possible contacts that could help with the project as most of them had children on the spectrum, and these people attended various different autism trainings., which meant they were knowledgeable. Kathy connected with these people, started an autism squad, which was initially nine members. Everything started moving towards a purpose.

She had no idea that this service was direly needed within her community. She had no idea how much help local parents needed for their children who were suffering from autism. There wasn't a possible setting for these parents to go to in which they could seek help. To add to her surprise, the community had nothing to offer, and she was going to take a step that would create a significant difference not just for her, but for countless lives within the community and beyond.

After the squad was formed, they had the chance to conduct the first meeting, and numerous parents showed up. They filled out a questionnaire so that the squad could gauge the problems that the parents were facing. This was back in 2018. Today, this small effort has ensured 95 children/siblings and family members that became part of the project and support system.

GRATITUDE – THE GAME CHANGER

The following year, the world came to a halt, and things took an unprecedented turn. She had caught an illness in September, and that is where she found yet another door opening for her from God.

A property that was located right next door to her home went up for sale. This property was special as it had a massive barn on it, stretching to 20.29 acres in size. She bought that in December 2020, and used that to kick-start another non-profit venture with two of her sons, and named it the Yocum-Brady-Cole Foundation. This was to serve as the home to Autism Acceptance in Cumberland County, IL. This is yet another amazing door that God opened up for her. She had always wanted to fulfil her dream, her life, and what her perseverance, consistency, determination, and her gratitude fetched her was a legacy that will be remembered for generations to come. After Kathy, her sons will take over, operate this organization within the state of Illinois, where they will establish a special needs training center. This will be where families of local schools can bring their children in, and be a part of the training facility.

She has already laid the foundation of such a huge, continuous project. She defines all of this as her one and true goal in life. For someone who had a rough start at life before entering adulthood, she is a living example for millions of lives to learn from, to be moved by. Stories like hers reinstate the concept of humanity, humility, and gratitude, and it is because of people like her that the world continues to draw inspiration to do something good

Throughout her journey, she has never been the one to expect any benefits or gains for herself, not even on a microscopic level. She has always put the needs of others before her own, and gives her all to give back to the community. That is what defines a leader, and that is what gratitude is all about. She knew she had the foundation to achieve her dream. She didn't stop there. She used that drive, that passion as fuel to do much more in life, all of which would continue to benefit others. She wanted her leadership abilities to affect those around her in a way that they could improve their lives, and she would never ask for anything in return.

Kathy has always been a survivor. She comes from a family of nine, and that naturally means some hardships will follow. Despite her difficulties and teenage pregnancy, she went on to redefine her life, and only in the last few years, created a profound impact on her community.

"I'm taking on the grandma role. When presenting my story on stage, in Washington, D.C., I found out that 15 to 20 people had started an autism group within their community. It became a snowball effect, and it feels so great to know that I was able to do all of that and pave the way. I had no idea about autism before any of this ever happened and that further fuels my happiness and joy to know I was able to do something larger than life."

Kathy recalls the entire scenario, and how it could have been different. She says, "I found out about autism equipment through an ad. Had I opened up a book and found something about crutches, I might have done that instead."

What she has done is amazing and every door that continues to open up for her, since the start in 2017, has been a 'yes' all the way.

Being Thankful for What You Have

Having gratitude is a vital part of life. Not only does it allow you to become a better leader and person, but it fulfils the feeling of abundance. Kathy counts every one of the blessings she has in life, including the warm clothes on her back, growing up with a big family, having food on the table. This is what defines her. For her, gratitude allows her to be herself. She says, "I can finally be what God has put me on earth to be." She can go on to do so much for others, and through that, she is able to do more for herself as well. Even more humbling that she continues to tell the world that this was a combined effort and never takes full credit because of the support that she's had from the squad she helped create.

Leadership isn't about leading the way of giving motivational speeches, or doing anything on a grand scale. It's about the little things each day. You don't t have to start a non-profit to be a great leader. Leadership comes from within and gratitude is the vehicle that drives your leadership to the next level, allowing you to uncover more that you can do for your team and your community. Kathy stresses how much people within any community need help. Special needs teachers require so much assistance, equipment, and tools to get the job done. Autism chose her because of the absence of support within her community. She wanted to make sure autism was accepted within society, making 'autism acceptance' a household phrase through education.

She might have been barred from pursuing her dreams back when she was a teenager, and that feeling of not being fulfilled is what fueled her desire to ensure others do not feel the same way. She stepped up in a community that had nothing to give to families suffering from autism, and she created a role for herself within her community.

They say that if you can change one life and create a positive impact, you have secured eternal success. Kathy has already influenced, impacted and changed hundreds of lives within such a short period, and that is a rare accomplishment,

One of the gifts that she's been blessed with is the ability to make sound decisions. Making a decision is what has excelled Kathy forward. She always encourages others to decide on whether they wish to become a servant or a leader, and if they choose to do so, she says "I'll run with you the whole time, but you must make that decision on your own."

GRATITUDE – THE GAME CHANGER

Most pretend to be living in gratitude. They use all the right words, claim all the things, and it seems they are moving on the right path. If people truly allow gratitude to be a defining part of their lives, they would always find peace with both the good and the bad.

Many people spend an entire lifetime trying to figure out they are grateful for, and Kathy has met them. One morning, she received a call from a friend who wasn't feeling her best. Kathy said, "Sit down, have a cup of coffee." She went on to explain "that warm feeling that's going in, that's gratitude." She directed her friend I to think about what gives her that warm feeling in life, and instantly, the girl started getting answers. The call that started on a sour note, ended successfully with revelation and gratitude filling the air.

Every day, she gets to get a dose of gratitude, love and care from those whom she has been able to help. She highlights how a specific person sends a text every day, thanking her and prays she has a blessed day. These are simple acts of kindness, the true meaning of gratitude. Her role is to connect others and direct them in the right direction for resources and monthly meetings.

One act of gratitude is all it takes to change the lives of many, and there is no greater example that I can think of than Kathy. Despite the restrictions, despite the hardships that the world faces today, she continues to lead the way, as a beacon of hope, love and care for countless souls. Her dream will come to fruition because look at what she's been able to do already! I'm not saying this because I know her, or because she helped with my quest of spirituality, but because she is genuinely the kindest, warmest and sweetest person I have had the privilege of crossing paths with. Her leadership and her gratitude, continue to redefine the lives of many with each passing day. Looking at her, I know gratitude can serve me, and anyone else for that matter, more than we realize.

Amy Earle is a military spouse, mom of four, and Mimi of two. She is passionate about freedom, education, and entrepreneurism. She homeschooled all 4 of her children instilling a love of learning into each of them, while building several successful businesses. Her passion for excellence, leadership and vision has made her a successful entrepreneur and educator of thousands of men and women throughout the world.

Chapter 4

Family

By Amy Earle

"Everybody has greatness within."

At the center of every successful story lies the support, love and care of the family. Whosoever has a dream, that dream is never complete without a family. For Amy Earle, the case is no different.

Amy Earle, who is arguably the wisest, most organized person I have ever met in my life, is a military spouse. She is a proud mother of four children, and a 'Mimi' for two. She is the icon for many, and yet she remains the most humble and noble person on earth. Her passion for freedom, education and entrepreneurship is unrivalled and unmatched by anyone I have met. To give you an idea of just how much her core values mean to her, she went on to homeschool all of her 4 children, and that is beyond extraordinary, even by today's standards. She did so successfully while creating and establishing several successful business ventures. I have seen her in action, and I have seen her passion for excellence drive her to places most of us can only dream of. Her vision and leadership qualities have made her into this powerful, influential and successful entrepreneur that has gone on to inspire and motivate thousands of men and women across the globe. This means that if she says "family is important," it simply is, period!

When her kids were young, she realized that each of her children was special and unique, in their respective ways. She truly believes that everyone is born to be great, it is just a matter of finding the path to bring out the greatness from within. She did whatever she had to, not because she wanted to be more successful in life, but because she wanted her children to be able to achieve that greatness in life. Since there is no "one-size-fits-all" formula for greatness, it required dedication of the highest order, one that she was ready to deliver. She knew that if one child has strength in something, it does not necessarily mean that the others would share the same traits. Everyone has their strengths and weaknesses, and she was able to identify these right away. Just to ensure that her children could have the best environment to groom in, and later go on to become great, she had to make significant changes.

This is the reason she started homeschooling in the first place. She went on to discover a principle-based method, better known as leadership education. It was through that she learned a lot of techniques and tools that she could then apply at home and teach her children.

As she learned more about this model, she realized children need a role model to follow at home. She quickly realized that the age-old method and tradition of putting all the burden on children by setting significantly higher expectations, telling them what to do and what not to do, was flawed. This would limit the child's exploring mind, bind them to limits that they would then dare not to cross, and that would often mean that they would miss out on a lot of opportunities that would otherwise allow them to achieve success.

She learned that by becoming a role model for her children, she could portray all the strengths, confidence, and success, hence influencing the children to emulate her personality and traits themselves. By becoming a role model, we, as parents, become the person children follow. We go on to become the person that we want our children to become at some point in time. It is a fairly simple philosophy; if we want our children to have a great education, we must first acquire said great education ourselves. Only then will we be able to influence them, encourage them and lead them to the same position.

Amy often says, "If we want them to do our things, we need to do our things. If we want them to never quit, we don't have to quit." As simple as this may sound, it is quite a powerful way, but one that certainly requires a life-long commitment, dedication, and consistency. There is no point in doing everything right, by the book, for a year and then reverting to our original selves the following year. Once you start, there is no going back.

It was 2008 when Amy started her quest. Then, she was a stay-at-home wife. She found herself completely focused on her children. Soon, she realized that she had to live her own life fully, take risks, and take challenges. She knew she had to go out of her comfort zone, and she had to do all of this just to ensure that her kids had a perfect role model within her. At the end of the day, all she wanted was for them to say "our mom did it, and if she can do that, I can do that too."

Unlike what many would think, none of this was done in secret. She did not do all of that, hoping that one day her children would figure out what she was doing. Whatever she was doing, she made sure that her children noticed, and explained how the children would one day be able to do what their mother was able to do. Of course, there were bittersweet moments, sprinkled with success, joy, laughter, sadness, and even mistakes that made Amy burst into tears, but that was all a part of a journey she had commenced on.

Initially, Amy was only focused on home-schooling. It was only after learning about leadership education that she decided to make these changes. She could have chosen to allow her children to continue studying in regular schools, but this wasn't the kind of education she wanted her children to have. This wasn't the kind of education that would lead to the greatness that she believes everyone has.

The Beginning of a Change

Of the four children Amy had, one of her sons was never too sure if he was doing something right, questioned everything in life, and would suffer from severe anxiety. He was always looking for some kind of outside validation. This is where Amy decided to bring him home and home-school him. The focus was on him to ensure that he gets to feel good, that he can cope up with his education, and that he feels free. The year ended, and it felt like Amy had run straight into a wall. Both of them ended up hating each other. Even though the child was only in first grade, Amy came to a point that she decided to send the child back to school because it was not working for both of them.

During this time, as Amy decided to have her children go back to school, she came across a curriculum fair where homeschoolers could go, learn about all that is latest and in demand, and buy all the tools and equipment they need to ensure they provide updated knowledge to their children. For no reason, Amy's husband restricted her from paying a visit to the curriculum fair.

This may not come to most as a surprise, but she still ended up at the curriculum fair. Whether it was meant to be, or it was a sign from God, it happened. She went on to buy a single book, nothing more. The book was *Thomas Jefferson Education.* Little did Amy know that this book, which she had bought and brought home, would go on to change everything in her life.

She went on to read the book. The book clearly explained the potential that our children have. This book gave a completely new perspective to Amy, and it almost felt like God had conveyed his message to Amy. The message was clear, "Your children are worth what is going to happen." It taught her that they, the children, are worth fighting for and all the efforts that she would go on to put in would eventually produce results far more pleasing than she might have thought possible.

For the last 12 years, Amy has lived a completely different type of life. She would go out with her children, catch the local buses, hike the mountains, backpack, and always seeking out opportunities to do otherwise hard things. As this went on, the children were continuously being influenced by

Amy's new lifestyle on a subconscious level, and that was a major part of the training.

Not only that, but Amy also came to learn one simple fact; her life wasn't over. She had a lot more to give to herself. This new venture allowed her to see that she, as an individual, had a lot of potentials. Working on that, she then realized that her children had great potential too.

The reality is that parents cannot be with their children every step of the way. There will eventually come a time where children will grow into adults, and they will be making their own decisions regarding what to do with their lives. Amy, through the book that she picked up, learned that it wasn't just about the children either. She had to step in and teach them how to think and what to think. She had to be that role model that the children can look up to, learn from and be inspired by. For them to go on and achieve greatness, they had to be trained to adopt the right state of mind. They had to know how to solve a problem without always relying on their mother.

Amy defines that as the crux of leadership, and she isn't wrong. A leader, by definition, is one that can help people get on the right track, make the right choices, and gain the confidence to pursue success. As a leader, it is up to you to know and figure out how you will decide, what you will decide and when, without relying on others because, the fact is, others are already looking up to you for guidance. If you do not have the answers, they will feel lost and clueless.

What Amy started doing, helped not only her children, but it helped her become the kind of leader that she is today. Through her experiences, quest, and venture, she has come to learn so much, which is why she can teach thousands of men and women how to become a great leader and a terrific role model for the family to follow.

"You are the expert in your home."

This is the first thing that Amy teaches everyone, and it is true. It may not be the best for you, but it is better than someone else stepping in and telling you what you must do for your home. You, as a parent, spouse, and family member, are the expert. You get to decide and choose what will happen within your home. You are the person in charge who gets to decide what is good for you and your children. Your children have been given to you as yours. This automatically makes you the steward over them.

When God grants you such a status, He empowers you to do it well. There is no room for failure because God does not set anyone up for failure. We, through our mistakes and ignorance, run into failure. God wants us to excel in life, to lead as an example for our family and children first before we could go on to lead for the rest of the world. Change starts from home and then flows outward. Therefore, it is up to us to be wise stewards of these great blessings. It begins with trust, where your children will trust you to be their leader. After that, it is just ensuring that we get the right tools and knowledge to help fulfil the vision and lead with full preparation.

Every leader, every entrepreneur and successful person on earth has a mentor, and that is a fact that no one can deny. It is through these mentors that people get to learn how to lead in life, how to be a better version of themselves, and how to move forward when all roads seem to lead to a dead-end. As parents, that role of a mentor falls on to us. For our children, we are the mentors, meaning that we are bestowed with a responsibility that would help shape the future of our children.

There is a significant difference between having a teacher or a professor and having a mentor. People often use these terms interchangeably, but that is wrong. Both have different purposes that they serve. A mentor is someone who knows us individually. It is a mentor that helps us become the best version of ourselves, meaning that they would encourage us to identify our strengths and weakness, work on these, follow our passion, change our lifestyle choices, and lead as an example. On the other hand, a teacher is one who knows us as a student in a class. They would teach everyone the same thing, without taking into consideration what a person may be passionate about, and what their strengths or weaknesses may be.

Amy owns a photography business, and this is yet another example of her setting benchmarks for her children. She started this business just to be able to show her children how it is done. For the people in that business, she would hold workshops where the show would teach everyone how to use a camera and take pictures accordingly. That is Amy as a teacher. As a mentor, on the other hand, she would be asking people questions on what kind of photography they are interested in, what their passion is, what their strengths are, and so on. These are two completely different roles, and the sooner this confusion ends, the quicker people can benefit from it.

Through her experience, Amy was able to become a mentor to her children. By asking questions about their strengths, passion, interests, she was able to provide each of her children different education, and there was a very good reason for that as well. Each child was taught about subjects that were in line with their passions and goals. She did not impose anything upon her children that were not a part of their passion, ensuring that the children never feel burdened by matters they were not interested in or were unable to understand. By doing so, it is no longer a conveyor belt that continues to produce the same kind of people with the same kind of education. It now becomes a purpose-driven method that works.

It is through this that Amy learned that she, herself, had a purpose, a mission and that she had to play her part as well. She quickly realized that she could not speak about purpose and mission to her children unless she knew and worked on her missions and purposes. It is only then that her children would get to learn the core values and be able to pursue the kind of greatness that Amy knows a believe they are blessed with.

Amy is proud to know that her children are now fully confident and clear on who they are meant to be, and are ready to go out into the world and conquer their dreams and ambitions.

For many, life kind of ends when they are married and have kids. This is especially true with women, but here is Amy telling the rest of the world that there is always a way to continue to grow. Amy was able to regain her life, seek out her mission and fulfil her purpose, and all because she chose to be a leader for her children and her family. It goes to show that life never really ends unless you decide for it to do so. If you have the will, passion and commitment, there is no reason why you would not go on to live your dreams and set yourself as a role model for your family and others to draw inspiration from.

Amy claims that while she imparted knowledge and expertise to her children, they also imparted the love of learning to her. The entire process taught her why one should never stop trying to grow into a better person. Through reading books, doing research, and finding something new to learn, Amy was able to change her life completely. It affected her and her family positively, allowing every one of them to become the best versions of themselves, and it is all thanks to Amy who bravely decided to take risks, accept failure, and learn. For Amy, the very idea of growth is non-negotiable. Of the 5 core values that Amy had in life, growth is one of them, and it shows just how significant of a role it plays in her life.

Knowing Your Values

A significant number of people in life tend to live their complete stay on earth, and for the best part of their lives, they have no idea what their core values are. Surprised, right? If you walk at any street of your choosing, and you talk to a stranger and ask what their core values were, I assure you that most would immediately go silent.

For Amy, she had already done her homework, and that is a part of the many reasons why she is who she is today. For her, her core values take priority over everything else. Any true leader would go on to say the same, and it is easy to see why. These core values, whatever they may be, go on to directly affect us, our behavior and our lifestyle choices. It is because of these core values that we get to know what is right for us and what isn't.

Amy has five core values that she prioritizes in life. She has done a marvelous job at ensuring that these core values are never jeopardized, ignored or overlooked. Her core values are:

1. Freedom
2. Growth
3. Awareness
4. Impact
5. Love

Freedom

Amy uses her values as a foundation and bases all of her decisions and choices using the said foundation. Think about these values as the exoskeleton of a body. Depending on the kind of exoskeleton, how its shaped, and what features it has, a body can then be attached to it to give it a proper shape. For Amy, her values serve the same purpose. All of her decisions, answers, choices, and thoughts must align with her value. They must fit the exoskeleton, and if they don't, they are simply discarded.

Of all the values, she values freedom the most. For Amy, freedom comes from her husband, who has served in the military for over two decades. Her freedom to speak, her freedom to choose what is best for her and her family, all of that matters a lot.

Growth

It is the idea of personal development that essentially means to continue and learn something new every day. It is an idea that propels Amy to do something new, something different and something productive that helps her grow as a person, an individual, an entrepreneur, and a mother.

Awareness

This is where Amy's faith comes in. The awareness of herself, awareness of God, awareness of relationship and everything in the middle, all of that falls under awareness. Amy uses awareness to know if her actions are in line with her goals of serving God, serving the community and helping those who need help.

Impact

Amy analyzes all of her thoughts, actions, visions and goals, just to see what kind of an impact it might have on those around her, especially her family. If the impact is good, she would not hesitate to act, but if it is anything other than that, she would walk away without giving it a second thought.

Love

This is quite self-explanatory. Amy prioritizes her love for her family, for her community and everyone in general. She would always ensure that her actions, whatever they may be, are in line with this value, allowing her to do good for the people out of nothing but love and respect.

The End Result

One of the greatest gifts that come from living a life based on mission is that it allows each person to live their best life. Yes, there was a time where things weren't working well for Amy and her kids, but following her core values, putting them into action, and then making the decisions that she did in life, everything improved significantly. Today, everyone within Amy's family shares a strong bond. There is strong and clear communication between each of these family members. It is worth noting that her kids are no longer kids, and despite their ages, having such a strong and healthy bond is a sign that things have worked out well for Amy and her family.

They get to spend quality time together. They get to talk about hard things and the joys of life. It was only possible because Amy chose to fill the shoes of a leader in the house. She is the person who stepped up and went on to achieve that role-model figure within the family, allowing her children to have all the inspiration they need at home.

Of course, the entire process took years in the making. It is only natural that she often felt slightly worried about whether this effort of hers would fetch the kind of results she wanted, or if it will all go down the drain in the end. She continues to trust the process, and things eventually turned out far greater than she had anticipated.

Trusting the process is one aspect that people often forget, and end up losing their confidence and trust. This would ultimately mean that they would walk away from their years-long efforts, without actually realizing how close they were to their ultimate goals. It is natural that people question the process, think that it may not be working, or even rationalize that they are not "cut out for this." However, Amy stresses that for one to succeed in life, especially with family, one must continue to trust the process. It is that consistency that ensures they will achieve a breakthrough in life.

It is just like walking on a path that you know will lead to glory, but three-quarters of the way, you find yourself facing a bricked wall. If you were to give up now, all your efforts would be in vain. However, if you continued with your momentum and consistency, that wall will eventually break, allowing you to complete the rest of the journey and reap the fruits of your hard work.

Each of Amy's child continues to take a step forward in the right direction, hence filling Amy with reassurance, confidence and pride. They can do amazing things at such young ages, and that only goes to show that they will, one fine day, go on to realize their dreams and goals in life. Everything worked out because Amy made it possible. Had it not been her choice to step out of her comfort zone and restart living her life to the fullest, just to allow her children to learn from her, none of this would have been possible.

Chapter 5

Faith

By Amy Earle

"We are born with a mission."

It is a little-known fact that faith and leadership go hand in hand with each other. Amy is a perfect example of a person who truly uses both of these to not only reach newer heights but to also become a leader that is unlike any other.

Since everyone is born with a mission that is assigned by God, everyone has a role to play in this life. Everyone has a purpose that they must seek out in life, and fulfil. God knows us, and who we are, and what we can do. He has placed within us the greatness that we can go on to achieve through fulfilling our purposes to the maximum of our capabilities.

When we can recognize that we have all these talents, traits, and skills, we must know and have faith that we will go on to play our roles accordingly. Yes, it may be a little too spiritual, but that is what defines her.

There are three specific principles that Amy goes on to teach her children, her family, her students and her business. These principles are:

1. We need to ask
2. We need to listen
3. We need to act

These principles came into her life back when she started her business in 2018. Additionally, she had picked up on a technique that Earl Nightingale spoke about, which essentially involves using a piece of paper to write down what one is grateful for, and then writing the following scripture on the back:

Ask, and it shall be given to you
Seek, and you shall find
Knock, and it shall be opened unto you

What Amy had developed using this technique, she recognized how she could ask for something and have faith that it will come in her life. Call it a miracle, or fate. It worked for her, and it helped her become a better person, a better leader.

However, there is more to it than just asking. There is also the principle of listening. Once you have asked, you now have to go another step further, and that is where listening comes in. After asking, you must set aside time every day, and pay attention to what comes in as an answer. So how do you listen to something that you just asked for? Simple – Your thoughts!

God has mysterious ways to communicate with us, to show us possibilities, opportunities, and grant us what we asked for. Thoughts are one way through which we can learn what we must do, and that, right there, is essentially God's will to incept that thought within you. If God wants you to do something, or have something, He will show you the way to acquire it. You may be clueless about how you can go on to become successful in life, and all it takes is that one thought, one light-bulb moment that will change the course of your life for the better. That's God telling you what you are supposed to do, seek out and pursue.

Finally, once you have figured out what needs to be done, whether to move ahead or ignore a scenario, you then act upon it. It is needless to say that we may often ask for things we think might benefit us, but God knows best. If something isn't good for you, He will fill you with thoughts that will take your mind off such a thing, and in its place, He will show you a path to something even better. That's God, and that's how much He cares. All of this, however, hinges around your faith.

If you can find it within yourself to have faith in the process, to have faith in your abilities, your mission and purpose, you will eventually go on to discover ways through which you will not only make it to the end, but you will do so in grand style.

When it comes to business, we often feel that we need to get something done, because it feels so good of an idea to miss out. Before you know it, a name pops up in your head, and you instantly know you are on to something. This could be a name for a product, a service, or the name of your future brand or company. However, many tend to overlook and ignore such thoughts that pop in, hence barring themselves the possible benefits that could have come their way had they acted on their thoughts accordingly.

It is God who goes on to give us these inspiring ideas, and He does so because He only wants the best for us. Of course, it may not be the end of things because there are times where He will test you, and He will use you till the end before dispatching a life-altering reward your way. At the end of it all, we are only playing a part we were born to play, whether we know it or not.

Act Now or Forever be Silent!

When these inspirations come Amy's way, she never hesitates and acts almost instantly. She goes on to work on these ideas, figure out how they could be used, and that always allows her to move forward positively. Depending on the type of idea that she comes up with, she would speak to the relevant person, arrange an event, write it down and post it to her wall, brimming with notes, or any other action that she deems necessary. All of this action puts something greater at work in motion. The wheels start turning, and before anyone knows it, she is rolling towards her goal.

"Every inspiration has an expiration."

Pause for a moment, and take in the wisdom that Amy's quote has to offer. It is one of the most overlooked concepts, and one that often leads people to wonder "I did what was needed, how did I manage to fail?"

Every thought, every inspiration that comes your way, comes with an expiration. If you act on these thoughts and inspiring ideas in time, you will most likely go on to achieve the success of some kind. However, if you delay matters, thinking that you can always pick up on that idea, later on, know that you are allowing someone else to utilize the same idea before you. By the time you decide that it is time, you are already too late.

Quite often, people think that if things are meant to be, they will happen sooner or later. The fact is that God tests us at every turn. He throws something your way just to see if you can act on it. Of course, these may not be breakthroughs all the time, but if you cannot act for a small scale of success, you certainly cannot expect that God will shower you with anything more significant. Amy firmly believes that to achieve success, we must prepare ourselves, make ourselves worthy for it. Make no mistake, everyone is worthy, but only those who actively go on to claim the prize. It is the fulfilment of the purpose that God tasked you with which brings forth rewards of unimaginable magnitude, and if you tend to ignore these signs, not act on time, and take things easy, someone else will be granted the task, and it will still be done; just not by you!

How Amy Defines Faith

Certainly, there is the religious side of affairs, but faith is not just limited to that. Faith is knowing that there is a higher power that is ruling everything, granting those who fulfil their roles the success and joys of life they desire, and it is also knowing that our endeavors, consistency, perseverance and commitment will pave the way for success to come out. It is trusting God and the process that He has created for us to follow.

"Faith is taking the first step, even when you can't see the whole staircase."

Martin Luther King Jr.

It is through faith that one develops the power to have a vision. A vision that can go on to define what kind of scenarios, success, choices, and lifestyles they expect to see at the end of their struggle. It is this vision that drives us forward, allowing us to create our success. Amy says that God can do whatever He wills, but He will not do everything for us. He wants us to take the lead and get the job done. If that wasn't the case, none of us would be working our brains out, trying to make something meaningful out of our lives.

Our visions, however different they may be, direct us to move in particular directions. They go on to influence our decision-making process, guide us when we feel lost, and provide us with a sense of purpose, and it is through our efforts and dedication that we eventually go on to meet our success. The only part that remains is to connect the dots from here to there, and that is where we need all the faith we can find.

"You can't connect the dots moving forward; you can only connect them looking backwards. So, you have to trust that the dots will somehow connect in the future."

Steve Jobs

Amy explains that there is no way you can tell if these dots are connecting until you get to the point in life where you want to be. That is where it will all make sense, and that is where the grand plan that God has in store for you will be revealed.

Back when she was raising the children, she wasn't too sure if any of her efforts, the homeschooling, the leadership education, would work. Now, after everything is done, she can confidently tell that these dots connected, and she can guide others on how she was able to do just that. Now, as a director, and a leader, she can tell others how she did that. Had anyone asked her how she was going to do it, she would have been clueless. It was pure faith that led her to continue doing what she was doing, hoping and believing that these dots will one day connect. Sure enough, after she reached her goals, she was able to connect these dots and figure out how each of these dots was connected.

It takes three aspects that, when combined, deliver you the results you seek. These are:

1. Faith in God
2. Faith in yourself and your capabilities
3. Faith in the process

Miss out on the first two, and you will most likely miss out on the last one as well. The lack of faith is evident in people who go on to try something today, and hope for results to pour in tomorrow. The next day, when the results do not come in, they simply give up the idea thinking "well, that doesn't work," and that would be the end of that.

The lack of faith is also what reinforces ideas like:

- It doesn't work
- I am not capable of doing this
- I can never be a leader
- I can never succeed
- I am bound to fail

All of these are far too common and can be witnessed almost every single day. That is the lack of faith talking.

Faith is far more powerful than most people care to realize. It is that beacon of hope that will eventually shine for you, just like it would shine for a ship that is lost in the wilderness of the seas for ages. That ray of hope, when it does come, changes everything. It is our faith that pushes us to continue doing what we plan on doing, being consistent, showing up every single day and work towards the goal. None of that is possible without faith because once you take faith out of the equation, you are left with nothing but concepts that you can neither work with nor act on. Why? Because your lack of faith will question these and will keep you bouncing around without consistency or commitment.

Everything in life is hard. Whether it is raising a family, securing a job, starting a business, seeking higher education, all of that needs commitment and faith. People often say that faith just doesn't work, but that is them giving up far too soon. If faith would not have worked, people would have stopped educating their children completely. The only reason they go through years of hard work is to ensure that their child can go on to attain a degree and land a decent job. That 'hope' is faith in the process of educating the child, getting them enrolled in a prestigious institute, and one day seeing their child get a job that pays well. Despite clearly exercising faith, quite a few continue to overlook how faith was able to hold them steady throughout the rough times, and it is because of their steadfast nature, consistency, commitment and dedication that they eventually get to see the results they were hoping for. That is faith coming back to reward them.

Vision

The stronger your vision, the more committed you become. Imagine taking a drive from the East coast to the West coast. It is arduously long, cumbersome, tiring, mammoth of a task to do. Then, there is the possibility of running out of gas, feeling drowsy, having a flat tire, or even running into other scenarios that may cause you discomfort. However, if you can visualize your destination vividly, clearly and with intent, you will change the flat tires, you will get your car filled up with gas every time it needs a refill, and you will drive through thousands of turns that you have no idea about, just to make it to the destination. That long and painfully tedious task that you started with will end with you relaxing at some beach on the West coast. That is only because you genuinely wanted to fulfil your vision. The bit in the middle is where your faith will come into play. The idea of "I will drive for as long as I have to, just to reach there," is faith talking, and it will get you to your destination sooner or later. Your faith kicks in right from the start, and it was because of your faith that you created a vision for yourself to drive thousands of miles, just to relax a little. It is this faith of "I am worthy" and "I can do this" that ensured your success in the end.

Being able to visualize your vision, your goal and your destination make a lot of difference. This is why many successful entrepreneurs take time out to visualize their success, their day, and their year. They do so because "seeing is believing." Once you can see everything clearly and visualize it, you start having a stronger faith in yourself, God, and the process that is involved. You start taking action accordingly because now, your vision is what is leading you towards your goal. It is this vision that pulls you through, motivates you and encourages you to carry out the action that is required.

Everyone has a calling in life and blessed with opportunities. It is up to each one of us to grab these opportunities and act on these while having faith that it will one-day work miracles for us If you procrastinate, someone else will take upon these tasks and get them done. God's work cannot go undone, which is why it is a choice we must make. We can either be the ones to get the job done, act on these opportunities and visions, or we can be the ones to see how someone else goes on to grab the same opportunity and reap the fruits that could've been ours. Somebody has to do it; let it be you!

Faith, or belief, is a muscle and everyone has it. The only difference is that some choose to exercise it while others are either intimidated or just not using the muscle. When a muscle is out of practice, it hurts significantly the first time you put such a muscle to use. This is exactly why people who go to the gym experience the first time they lift weights, or run, or do push-ups. It happens because these muscles were never

FAITH

used before and now, they are taking on heat and stress the kind of which they have never experienced before. Let's face it there has to be a first time and you don't know what you don't know. After a while, that hurtful feeling vanishes, and what people end up with is quite literally an addiction. It becomes second-nature to use that muscle that once remained dormant.

    It is through exercising your belief, or faith, that you create an extraordinarily strong vision. By continuing to work towards your vision, believing in it, and being consistent, a day will come when that vision will manifest itself for you.

Jennifer Pavlick is an entrepreneur, retired hairstylist, proud Mama and military wife from Dane County, Wisconsin, who has a great love for her dogs and her award-winning show horses. She has an inherent passion for helping people and loves inspiring others to find their internal strengths and works to guide them towards being the best versions of themselves. Her truest happiness is when she can help others harness their desire to be of service to others through the education of healthy lifestyle patterns.

In her free time, Jen lives for interior design and home remodel projects with her husband, Steve. Additionally, Jen adores the outdoors and spends as much time outside as possible, in every one of our Wisconsin seasons. Notably, Jenn loves fishing, skiing, shooting at the range and ample time lifting weights at the gym.

Chapter 6

Leading Yourself

By Jennifer Pavlick

"I am a fixer. I want people to succeed because if people are happy, I am happy."

This is one of the most profound things I've heard, considering the kind of world we live in today. These are not my words, but those of the incredible Jen Pavlick. I have met a significant amount of great people in life, some of whom you have already read about, and Jen Pavlick is another gem that I am honored and blessed to have met.

She is an inspiration not just to me, but virtually to everyone who has ever had the chance to get to know her, or even hear her speak. She is a successful entrepreneur, a loving mother, a perfectly imperfect wife, and she hails from

Wisconsin. While she is all of that and more, she is the kind of person that is rare.

For anyone of her caliber, intellectual level and character, it is rare to see people like that care immensely about others and they are willing to put their dreams on hold, just to ensure others get a chance to become the best versions of themselves first. The quote you read at the top isn't just to win you over; she truly lives to see others succeed in life.

Besides being involved in network marketing, much more, she fills her time with health and fitness, raises show horses, is a dog lover and a busy farmgirl. She also owned her own business for over twenty-five years. Her passion lies in so many different arenas.

Passion defines her. Passion to show people all they can offer to the world, just by being the best version of themselves, and she doesn't stop there either. She's a confidence builder, and helps them to take the first step towards a transformed life, one that ultimately leads to success, the that they never thought they'd see.

As a salon owner, Jen's job was to overlook her own problems in life to listen to the problems that her clients were having. She delivered advice and served her clients. Each of her clients would walk in and pour their heart out, and she would be the one to give them advice that was relevant. Upon witnessing this pattern, she figured out soon enough that she

LEADING YOURSELF

was a good adviser/coach, and that she has this amazing gift of guiding people through their problems, and allow them to not only feel good while looking good (because your hair is the crown you never take off) and confident enough to pursue a higher quality life. For the advice she gave, she could help change someone's life for the better - that's where she was happy. It moved her, and it gave her a purpose. She feels good about being able to contribute to someone else's life and basked in the positive outcomes That, for all intent and purpose, was just the start of a journey she would embark upon.

She noticed that people would come to her with an issue and then seek help, or they would come to her with their issues, when they needed a compassionate ear. Her goal is always to open up their eyes to the greatness they have within. No matter how great of advice she gave, no matter how confident she was with her words and wisdom, she always felt there was a part of the confidence that was missing. Despite everything she was doing, she felt like she wasn't doing enough to lead, and she knew there was plenty more room for her to work on herself.

It wasn't long before she received what she hails as the best advice she has ever received.

"If you're going to be a leader, lead yourself!"

This advice instantly clicked with her. It opened a completely new scope for her to explore. She realized that she could inspire people, motivate them and provide them with the tools they would need to succeed in life, but they e will still follow her as their leader. With time, she understood that everyone, despite having all of that, will still follow your lead and that you can never do the work for them. She led by providing them with everything they need to step forward, effing simple right? Whether they choose to work or not, that's a completely different question.

Jen believes that the same applies to personal life as well. She explains that if someone wishes to be a leader, they have to be one both on and off the field. Many people may be great with financial and business advice, but they may not have the best advice out of these areas of expertise. Naturally, we all come with our strengths and weaknesses, but as a leader, that is simply the case. Identifying where you can grow as a leader and what you need to outsource is very important.

A leader must be someone who is advising that they, as individuals themselves, will be ready to implement the same tools. Nobody should be directing their team if they're not going to do the same work. Jen ensures that she only gives out advice to other people that she would be willing to use for her own business or personal matters.

LEADING YOURSELF

She has developed notable respect for people around her and within her community. She believes that the respect she carries for people, influences their everyday life, and that is what a true leader is supposed to do. Leadership doesn't end with Jen being a great source of advice for business, but she believes that she should take a step further and help them out in their everyday life as well. Make your people feel important. Celebrate the micro-wins because over time those add up.

Some may have their businesses running successfully and smoothly, but if their state of affairs outside the world of business is in tatters, they need help. She has always been a firm believer that she should do whatever she can to help fix issues, which is why she calls herself the 'fixer.' Yet she knows it's up to the individual to fix themselves.

It isn't just about Jen giving her precious advice either. The party on the receiving end must also be willing to apply sage advice and knowledge in their lives, both professional and personal. People must be willing to take accountability and hold themselves accountable for their actions, and the amount of work they're putting in towards their goals and objectives. They must be willing to do the work to get there and reflect on how much they have done right, and what they may have done wrong. This is what leads to personality development.

For anyone who is aspiring to be a leader of a team and one that performs, know that leadership isn't a smooth ride. It can get sloppy at times. Anyone can be a leader as long as they can apply themselves, utilize their skills properly, and be willing to face the challenges that come their way. You can't expect to be a leader overnight either. It's a process that involves you to take one step at a time, one foot after the other. It takes time, but it is so worth it. As a leader, you must be willing to always grow.

If something doesn't work out right, there's no need to sugar-coat it. Be transparent about what has transpired, learn from it and accept it. Seek advice from your mentor, reflect upon your decisions, visualize your goals and find out how you can improve upon the given situation or task.

She emphasizes the fact that while one needs to respect others and counsel them, it doesn't mean that the complaining should continue. While coaching others, one must respect the line between personal life and business. If someone has a bad day, it's perfectly okay to talk about it, but dragging it any further, or being stuck with it is just not productive Instead of focusing on all that went bad, acknowledge that it happened, and then start counting the blessings and make an action plan to change what isn't working.

Nothing in life is perfect, and leaders, however successful they may be, are no exception to that. We all have had great days, and we have had some of the worst days. It's a natural part of life that we can't ignore, avoid or overlook. This is why you will never see successful leaders tell others that their life is perfect. They are transparent about the challenges they had and the action steps that they took. Now and then, leaders must be willing to do the things others are not willing to do, and that may often mean getting their hands dirty, finding themselves in uncomfortable situations or facing overwhelming challenges. Identify the issue, present solutions and act. That is a part of leadership, and that is effectively a test that every leader must go through more often than not. Those who are intimidated, simply vanish. Those who go through the problem, come out as better leaders.

They'll Seek Advice

For someone with 26 years' worth of business experience, Jen explains that people will come to you for advice. They will tell you anything and everything as long as you're an effective listener. Even older generations still want advice from her, just because they know she's always willing to help with direction.

She recalls a time where a client would come to her every 6 weeks and tell her the same thing over and over. Jen asked, "So what are we going to do about it?" This client would have the same problem and never wanted to break the cycle. Something was missing. Jen listened to her dilemma once again, but this time, she asked if they were going to continue this repetitive cycle, or if this time, the she would take a step to address the situation. Jen suggested to her that it was time to move ahead, take a step and resolve the issue once and for all.

This was the logical thing to do to hold her accountable and help her see that she DID have the confidence to break the cycle. Jen understood because she could relate to the situation that her own client was in, and Jen knows how powerful that one step is to take action. Complaining won't fix anything, only action will.

Leading Off the Field

Given her nature and success, people look up to her with respect and view her as a figure of authority. She is passionate about her family, excels in her leadership skills, and loves giving meaningful advice to those who seek her help. Of course, there will be those who may consider this leadership aspect as arrogance (which is actually confidence), but that is their limited point of view. If we start paying attention to the negativity, we will never be able to move forward and do what is right for us, our teams, and the world. As a leader, Jen considers herself as a vault; a vault and place your trust. She would never break that trust, not even for her husband. She firmly believes that trust is rare, and if you are capable of being trusted, you should do everything within your power to maintain it. By being trustworthy, she can lead not only on the stage and in the field of business, but she can replicate the same leadership off the field as well, which is why she has gone on to become the kind of leader that she proudly is today.

She emphasizes the importance of being a good leader off the field. This is something one must do to develop their relationship skills, leadership style, and earn respect from those you know When you can do that, you will naturally start attracting significantly more business, and your business will experience a lift-off that is both unprecedented and astonishing.

"It's not how you lead on the field that counts, it's what you do behind closed doors that does the trick."

Jen points out that everyone faces adversities in life. Leadership is about acknowledging these adversities and then finding the will to change the course of action and motivate others to do the same. Leadership lies in how you connect with others, help them see that change is not something to be intimidated by, but it is something that must be done to reach new peaks. There is no point in putting on a persona of a 'leader' on the stage and being a sore loser off the field. A leader is a leader in all aspects of life, which is why Jen is who she is both on and off the stage. She remains true to who she is, what she is and how she acts and does not put on a façade that others often tend to do. Life is messy and beautiful, and so is being a business owner.

    Jen has been able to enhance her business experience purely through transparency and honesty. By being her true self, she can set the right expectations, allowing clients and other businesses to work with her more easily. She often warns people not to fake things or show the world how flawless they are because things can, and will, get messy at times. Those who are posing to be someone they are not are always, they eventually expose themselves and people will realize that the person was nowhere as capable as they claimed to be.

    By being true to yourself, being who you are and embracing it, you will attract the right kind of people. There is a significant difference between attracting the right kind of people and attracting everyone in sight. The right kind of people will be the people who will provide you with value. They will bring out the best version of you, and they will either go on to be your mentors or improve their lifestyles by learning from you. The same goes for business because each member of the right audience will want to work with you, for you, besides you. It's just like natural selection working in your favor. On the contrary, attracting everyone would simply mean that you will surround yourself with a messy situation where negativity will flow in every direction. That is simply a waste of time, energy and resources.

Jen was inspired by many, and she wanted to follow their lead and learn to be a good leader. Her passion, commitment and dedication ensured that surpassed other leaders and create her own substantial organization. She admits that it often hurts, but it is a part of life to outgrow others and then move on to find an inspiration that takes her to the next level. Through her path towards leadership, she learned that it is important to get to know how people respond to these changes. She started to realize that it was important to understand how people think, what motivates them, what scares them, and the more she learned this, the more she discovered that there was only so much that she can do for someone. If someone was not willing to change and make tweaks, it was serving no purpose to them or her.

Jen loves to highlight the gifts people hold within themselves. She does a lot to ensure that people find the courage to explore these gifts and make use of them, however, she can't force them to use them. As long as they're willing to listen, Jen can help them. For those who are unwilling, there is no amount of personal development that will help.

Lead Yourself

"What you do in your personal life reflects in your professional life. What you do in your professional life reflects in your personal life."

All of this is only possible once you know who you are, what your core values are, and can remain true to yourself. To be able to lead others, you must first lead yourself. You should be the one to ask yourself the hard questions and be able to come up with answers. You should be able to take a step forward and start with the process of changing yourself and developing yourself as a person.

Once you start leading yourself, not only do you find renewed confidence, motivation and a strong vision of what you want out of life, you will notice that you'll carry yourself differently. Your relationships improve and people start looking at you differently. You gain a completely new perspective on life, business, and the people around you. While all of these changes may intimidate some, they only need to take the first few steps to realize how much good lies once the switch is flipped.

Jen admits the downfall to wanting everyone to be happy, to be successful, and be able to pursue their dreams and make them into a reality - she gives more chances to people who may or may not deserve it. While Jen exudes forgiveness, not everybody is a go-getter, and many continue to exploit that nature, trying to seek out advice and counsel without ever showing the intention to invite change into their lives.

The ability to respond to a situation, to be able to take corrective actions, and to be able to work with the change, varies from person to person. They might get all the right advice and leadership from their mentors or friends, but if they do not respond accordingly, things can go from bad to worse.

The Challenges Leaders Face

You can read a gazillion books on self-help, and grasp every concept that is shared within these books. However, that knowledge will serve you with nothing unless you are willing to apply it in your own life. Unless you make a move, there will never be any personal development or growth to celebrate. It isn't just a matter of a day, week, month or year either. You will need to apply the knowledge that you gained, for the rest of your life, without breaking the momentum and consistency. It is through that hard work and application, when the growth and results really happen.

Oftentimes, people try to serve people too much, and there are just not enough giving back in return. The other scenario could be that people can resent just how much you are giving. That may seem surprising, but the fact is that some will simply make you feel shitty for giving so much. Either way, people have this unusual habit of taking you for granted, thinking that they will always turn back to you for every problem because... you guessed it! "You have the solution to every problem."

That may be true, but a leader is one who trains others to be leaders themselves, both on and off the field. They can try to train people before they are either able to see results coming out of it, or they decide there is simply nothing else that they can offer.

Of course, to some level, it does bother everyone what others think of them, and Jen is not immune to the negative feedback either. While she has an ability to withstand and endure negativity, there are times where she feels hindered by what others are saying about her. Just like anyone else, Jen has also hit rock bottom at one point in her life, but eventually, she found the will to start doing things for herself.

Once she started managing her own business, realizing that she needed to stop giving her energy to those without positive results, things started to move forward. She then started to take control of her action off the field, within her home and with friends, an extraordinary thing happened. Her business sky-rocketed, and her relationships improved significantly, and she has never looked back ever since.

Today, Jen leads her business and continues to inspire thousands of lives every single day. She has learned that people sit back and watch. If they trust you on a personal level and feel that you are loyal and accountable in your everyday life, they will be more apt to do business with you and work with you. She is the kind of leader that does what she says and says what she does. You have to lead YOURSELF every day on a personal level, just like Jen.

Sara Reed is a hairstylist and entrepreneur from Dallas, Tx. She's a wife, mother and part time aerialist. Her favorite thing about the network marketing industry is the opportunity it provides to help other people transform their financial futures.

Chapter 7

Courage

By Sara Reed

"Courage is not the absence of fear, but the triumph over it."

Nelson Mandela

Courage is one of the most important traits of a leader, to follow and Sara Reed exemplifies that is truly unique. What she has been through, and her ability to take that and insert into her business practices to take her from her lowest point to her highest is a true inspiration.

Sara Reed is from Dallas, Texas. She is a loving wife, an amazing friend, a mother and a part-time aerialist. I'm so grateful she said yes to telling her story in hopes of relating to even more readers - it's an honor that she is a part of this.

The Phoenix Rises

It is said that every phoenix has the incredible ability to rise back from the ashes, renewed and reborn. While I have not seen any phoenix to say for certain if that was the case, I have seen Sara do the impossible!

Eight years ago, Sara had reached rock bottom t in her life. She was caught in a malicious cycle of addictions, and her world was spiraling down, virtually out of control. This obviously is a hard place to bounce back from - it's no picnic. She worked extremely hard, mentally and emotionally to get to the place she is today. What's more amazing, is that she uses that dedication and those tools in her life and business today. It's rare to meet such an individual.

Her struggles often left her hopeless and clueless. For most of her life, she had no idea how to handle these challenges that she was facing. However, something within said enough is enough. That gave her renewed courage and she decided that she was going to do all that was required of her to come out of this void and become sober again. This alone is one of the scariest and hardest decisions that anyone can make.

That commitment and courage that she found, helped her to pull herself out of addiction. She often reflects on the moment she found the courage to take the step and change

COURAGE

things for herself and always finds an unlimited supply of courage to do greater things in life. She says:

"If I had the courage to get sober, and really deal with my feelings, with life, and getting it together, I can overcome anything."

There was a time Sara would easily refuse and say no to pretty much everything, but with the renewed spirit and newly-found courage, she found herself saying 'yes' to more things in life. She was no longer the kind of person who would doubt herself or her abilities. The prospect of "I can't do that" was no longer an option for her. She would look at her goals and face them head on, and she would tell herself that if she wasn't the kind of person who could achieve X, Y, or Z, then who can?

This renewed spirit within her pushed her forward, allowing her to say yes to one thing after another. Because it is effing simple, she decided. This created a person who was no longer someone that was devoured by the negativity and unhealthy habits. She had risen out of the ashes and become a powerful, inspirational and courageous woman who was ready to prove to the world that she could do anything she set her mind to.

Later, she said yes to yet another opportunity. With a little bit of courage, and a bit of investment, she embarked on a life-changing path that she did not know would become something larger than life for her and her family. She became a leader to her team, a leader of a multi-million dollars organization and grew exponentially herself. Sara was certainly shocked by how different life before that was for her.

"If you would have told me back then when I had started my business, that I would be responsible to lead others, I would have said no."

She recalls she wasn't sure if she could lead herself, let alone lead others. A brief moment of brevity helped her to do exactly that.

Sara emphasizes the importance of finding that courage to do something in life that scares you, even if it is just a fraction of courage. Anything great that happens in life is because of courage and bravery. No one is expected to show up with 100% courage, but if a person can muster up a small amount every day, and continue to do so, the compounding effect will surpass expectations. Courage brings change and making one courageous decision at a time will give you an endless number of possibilities and opportunities that open up for you.

Facing Your Fears

There is no denying that Sara was intimidated by the fear of the unknown. However, where many would have folded, she stood her ground and found the courage to move ahead with her decision to take on the opportunities that came her way. She knew in her heart that everything would work out. She says she jumped into the opportunity "blindly but courageously." The last 5 years, it has completely transformed who Sara is. She is now a person who can do things she never thought she could. She gained new skills. New doors opened. She discovered new talents and passions that she didn't realize she had.

Sara often goes back to some of her memories, just to reflect on where she started from, and where she is now. She used to be a shy introvert and wasn't the kind of person who wanted to be the center of attention. She preferred to sit back and observe the confident people that did want the attention.

A few years into her online business, she was asked to speak alongside a group of entrepreneurs and leaders to an audience of 8000 of her company's finest. Sara almost said no. She felt like she wasn't qualified enough to be on that stage, educating some of the most successful people in the industry. She felt like an imposter. Despite all that, she reminded herself that she was in fact courageous and said yes. She knew she had an impactful story to share. Her story is full of struggle and she knew there were others just like her trying to figure it all out. She said to herself. "Yes, I dare speak my own truth."

She went up on that stage and shared her story with full transparency. It was terrifying at first, but she let go, and let her soul do the talking. She was not on stage as someone she wasn't. She was up there for who she truly was. It was one of the most amazing moments of her life. A burden that had long been on her chest, was gone. She felt relieved, joyful, ecstatic, and full of confidence. It was all thanks to a fraction of courage that crept in at the right time and created an opportunity of a lifetime. Had she not had the courage; she would have missed out on that amazing experience.

The Many Faces of Courage

Courage has many faces. It can show up in so many different forms, far more different than the ones we read about in books, or watch on TV. You are a seed, and courage is the water and nutrients that you need to grow.

Reflection is a big part of Sara's life. She remembers masking her feelings with substances, pushing her to procrastinate in life and it could have gotten worse, fast. It came to a point where she became terrified of dealing with her addictions and the thought of being a normal person again. She did nothing but watch as others would drive to work, go to church, hang out with friends, and it came to a point where that was all she really wanted – a life!

The little mundane things that everyone takes for granted, like paying the bills on time, having a regular job, being able to laugh every once in a while, she wanted that. She had no clue where to start, and the idea of it was intimidating on its own and overwhelming. It was that little bit of courage that she eventually found within herself that gave her the energy and the will to say "Yes, I want that! I will do whatever it takes to clean up my mess."

Don't be fooled; the fear remains. However, once you break the ice and do something for the first time, such as Sara getting up on stage and speaking her heart out, things get easier. It's about practicing stepping out of your comfort zone. What opens up for you is room to enter the next level. Fear will always be there, but your courage and experience will say "Hey! We've done this before, and we can certainly do it again." You become the proof and validation to yourself that you can do things that you once thought were impossible.

Courage isn't always there. It is like a muscle or a skill. It is something that you have to work on every day, consistently, and intentionally. It is through the daily use of courage that you will develop more of it and utilize it. Don't stop being courageous or you'll sink back into mediocrity.

"I wasn't born as a woman with incredible courage. It was life that started depositing courage into my... courage bank account!"

It took time, but Sara was eventually able to draw courage from other sources and people when she needed it the most. Sara continues to push the boundaries further, trying to maximize her courage levels, so that she can be completely transparent about who she is, where she came from, and how she got through the obstacles thrown at her. She's been through challenges and disappointments, yet her only goal is to show others what facing courage can do to take those next steps.

The Courageous Leader

Courage is a vital part of leadership. Without it, one would simply not be able to make important decisions, and face valuable clients, customers, leaders and nay-sayers.

Sara has managed to master the art of courage, and she has successfully used it to transform her life and change it literally 180 degrees. She has inspired many that know r, and she continues to find the strength to go out and inspire more.

Growth of any kind is not a straight line. It is not a trajectory that you can plot on a piece of paper as a straight line. There are ups and downs, highs and lows, just like you see in the stock market. With every dip in life, courage is what allows us to create the next peak, to regain the lost ground and go even higher.

She is the kind of person who shares her own experiences to further highlight how others, who may be experiencing the same problems or issues and lacking the courage to find a solution, find it within themselves. Once you speak to another person who has gone through the same thing as you are experiencing, you tend to draw the same confidence from them.

"Courage is contagious. When a brave man takes a stand, the spines of others are often stiffened."

Billy Graham

It is simple; you cannot expect to help others unless you have experienced the same. It's up to individuals to decide when they are ready to take necessary actions, and until then, there isn't much that Sara, or anyone else for that matter, can do to alter their course of action. When they eventually do, she acts as their anchor for courage, allowing them to draw courage, inspiration and work their way towards their goals more productively and with purpose.

Standing Your Ground

Sara recalls how worried her family was about her, especially when she decided to close her salon and jump into a more lucrative opportunity. They would talk behind her back r, and some of them thought she was crazy. She could feel them waiting for her to fail. She used their doubt as fuel for her passion and commitment. She proved them wrong.

Eight years later, the girl who was misunderstood and underestimated, went on to make millions from her newly found passion and business. Today, Sara stands proud as a completely transformed woman, one that stunned, astonished and surprised not just her family, friends and business partners, but those who once thought she couldn't do even half of what she has been able to accomplish today. Now those doubters, send her messages telling her of how proud they are, and that she has found her calling.

I have known Sara for over five years, and I assure you; what she has been able to do is no less than a miracle. God has His way of choosing people through which He shows just how much possibility there is, and it is clear that He chose Sara for a bigger purpose than what she thought. She is a living and breathing example, the embodiment of courage. Without her contribution to this book, and to the lives of many, we would have never learned how true courage looks like and what it is capable of doing. Her words, her passion, and her story; will inspire people for generations to come.

Jennifer DeKezel

    I am 43 years of age and was raised in a small prairie town in Manitoba Canada.
    My heritage is Italian, Trinidadian and Venezuelan.
    I moved to the city of Toronto on my own when I was 18 years old. Since then I have worked very hard to survive, thrive and live my very best life.

This adopted child had always wanted a big house with lots of children and a family I could call mine. God had other plans for me.

Instead I am happily divorced, a mentor to almost 40 beautiful young girls in a program I started called Girlz Will Be Girlz, a foster mother taking in young girls and boys due to emergency circumstances and I am a proud Police Officer working as a Detective Constable for the Toronto Police Service.

My passions are my charitable work in the community, traveling and exploring in warm destinations, playing and watching sports, yoga and singing and dancing to any music, my favorite being country music. I am a foodie and lover of a good red wine.

I recently adopted a beautiful golden doodle puppy whom I named Bella, she instantly stole my heart.

I owe my life to my parents that raised me as their own since I was 3 months old and to my birth mother for unselfishly giving me up to ensure a better life.

I have 2 sisters and two brothers. I am also blessed with 2 nieces and 3 nephews.

I was raised with a high moral, to have integrity, loyalty and passion for whatever I do in my life. I have been faced with many forks in the road over the years, there has been some very rough patches and many moments that left me breathless and beyond grateful with my life and the beautiful souls that surround me.

My biggest love lesson is that you don't have to be blood related to love unconditionally and if you are ever in a situation where you question your next move, dig deep, use intuition, be patient, trust the journey and always lead with your heart.

Chapter 8

Integrity

By Jennifer DeKezel

For someone who never knew who her biological parents were, who was a darker skinned child raised by white parents, and who had gone through some of the worst possible nightmares, Jennifer Dekezel stands as a 5-foot powerhouse, an inspiration for millions of people in the world. She may not be tall, but never let her looks deceive you because she is a force to be reckoned with.

Her early childhood was filled with questions, she would seek answers to, but was simply unable to understand where to start, what to do and how to move forward., She would often question why she wasn't good enough if she was ever going to find her place within the society, and if she

INTEGRITY

would ever be accepted for who she is. Needless to say, she would always feel like an outcast. In the town she grew up in, she was surrounded by other white people, and this would create a psychological challenge for her to deal with, because she was different.

In most cases, some people would simply hide away from society, avoid going out, and would do whatever it took to avoid mingling with others, but not Jen. Thanks to her incredible parents, who taught her that being different was being special, she learned to accept who she was later in life. She found the determination and motivation to move ahead in life and never worry about how she was any different from anyone else. Now that she is in her forties, these life lessons helped shape her to be the leader she is today.

As she was growing up, she knew she carried sensitivity within her upon others:

Empathy- She was able to feel things that most people her age would simply overlook. For example, there were often times that she would see someone unable to have lunch at school because they weren't able to afford it or someone not feeling well. That helped her realize just how much of herself she could give to the world. She quickly started to find the passion within herself to become a reason for others to smile about, to be able to share smiles with them, care, and affection. She wanted to be someone who could do that and much more for others around her.

She recalls, "I could've taken a very wrong path, especially when I moved from Winnipeg to Toronto, Ontario. I didn't have anyone here that I knew. I had never lived anywhere else except farmland, and suddenly I was in the biggest city in Canada."

There, she found many things that were reprehensible, and they were absolutely against the principles and ideals that she grew up with and stood for. Had it not been for the values that were instilled within her by her parents, she would have led a completely different life today. Times were hard, and that meant that there were opportunities that came her way to make a quick buck, but not in any decent or legal ways, with zero integrity She decided that she'd rather not eat than do anything that went against her core values.

For anyone who is 18 years of age, those "dangling carrots" that are presented to people that come from struggle sound delicious. And unfortunately, many fall for the trap, without ever looking at the bigger picture that exists behind all of it. It was Jen's moral compass that barred her from doing anything that involved an act of indecency or immorality.

"I am fortunate to be alive. I am fortunate to be healthy. I am fortunate to not have a criminal record because I made the right decisions. I consider myself lucky and educated."

Her parents who gave her the best of everything, showered her with love and care, despite not being her blood family. Her mother taught her some of the most valuable life

INTEGRITY

lessons, one of which was to love others and receive love unconditionally.

Today, she gives away so much to young girls who have gone through tragedies of their own, lost families, or have been deserted. People often ask why she goes on to give these girls so much of her time and support, and the answer for her is always the same; she loves them, even if they're not hers.

Jen was raised in the country far away from all the guns and violence that you normally witness and hear about in the big cities. There were no threats or violence at large. It was all about having a perfect community, where everyone knew everyone. It felt nice, and it helped carve part of the personality that made her the way she is today. What she is trying to do is to replicate that loving and caring environment here. By being there, by giving so much of herself to these young girls, she is trying to ensure that they can go on to have a decent life ahead. Most of them have been exposed to a lot of violence, major crimes, they have gone through hell and back. By contributing to their lives, she can help create a difference.

Through all of this, she is trying to teach them how to better prepare themselves for the future., This is why she teaches these girls how not to take any dangling carrots.

She continues grow her foundation group, Girlz Will Be Girlz. She explains that a lot of these young women do not have both parents and are raised in a single-parent family where their parent is busy working tirelessly. They often do not find the full support they need, and that's when they are exposed to negativity out in the world. To help protect the community and ensure that citizens, especially young girls, to provide them with a more stable environment, help them to acquire a skill set to say no and make the right choices, she chose to become a police officer.

Jen has served in the worst precincts imaginable. She has firsthand experience with crime and violent activities some to brutal to even imagine.

"I know the details. I know the stats, and I know, without a doubt, it is very hard for these young girls."

Despite her tough job, despite all the hardships she may face, she continues to remain undeterred. She continues to help these girls out by mentoring them, by teaching them how to live a better, healthier, and happier life.

She teaches everyone to trust their instincts and intuition. Her way of explaining has helped many girls to become aware of what's right. This continues to help numerous lives and helps them save themselves from falling victim to heinous crimes, criminal activities and circles, allowing them a fair chance at a life that is more meaningful and fulfilling.

Integrity Matters

There is no denying that integrity matters especially when you are growing up. Having integrity is 99% of the success. People get to choose to decide. However, a child doesn't always have that option. To be able to lead a superior life, having a strong sense of integrity allows those to differentiate between right and wrong, to be able to make moral decisions. Often times children that are compromised rise out of the ashes and change the world. At one point in their lives, integrity was ingrained. It just takes one person to believe and to show support and that is the pivotal moment for a child.

Make no mistake; it's very tempting and easy to take a bite of the carrot. It seems easier to believe the story that someone is selling, but it is only after the carrot is accepted that these struggling young women realize what they've gotten into. It becomes virtually impossible to walk out of these situations, and that is why many who choose to make a quick fast money like this get sucked into these criminal circles. They are then controlled, used, and abused. One of the few outs is to never fall for the temptation. All that shines is not gold. The younger they are, the easier they become for predators to prey upon. These young girls struggle at school, live in low-income areas, have broken families and that usually is when these predators approach them and show them false dreams of making quick money and having someone "care.". They tell them how they would never have to worry about going to school again, and that they will be able to make so much money. Girls at this point are usually naïve, which is why they tend to fall victim.

They then push these students to an illegal lifestyle keep 'X' amount of profits, where X is still a significant sum of money for a person who is still in a school-going age. There are those who would entice these younger girls to sleep with adults and make money, and will claim that it will be fun and lucrative for them. These are professional groomers and know exactly what to say to these girls, how to manipulate and lure them to get them excited about leading a so-called 'luxurious' life that they could otherwise never dream of achieving. This is where Jen comes in, trying to remove these girls from such an environment where they could become prey. She gives her best efforts to ensure that these youngsters are exposed to reality and show a better life that is genuinely more rewarding. By allowing them to come out of their bubble, by showing them the world outside of the ones they are limited to, she is imparting knowledge and awareness, both of which serve key purposes in educating these youngsters. It is through these experiences that integrity develops and strengthens. It only takes one wrong decision that can ruin a good life forever with so much future ahead.

INTEGRITY

    Jen is providing her unconditional love, just to ensure that these youngsters, who come from strict poverty, abuse, and other problems of life, feel that they have someone they can look up to. She has seen firsthand how easily these youngsters can be approached by these carrot-danglers, and how easily they can fall victim to these crimes, and it is her mission to ensure that when such a time comes, these youngsters know exactly what they need to do.

    Every day, she ensures that these youngsters know that she will always be there for them, through thick and thin. People make mistakes, and Jen understands how youngsters are prone to do the same. Despite the mistakes, despite all that may be wrong, she always stands by them, is there for them, guides them and shows them.

    Jen has successfully changed the lives of 39 young women by doing what she does best. Those are 39 lives that will go on to spread her lessons, and guidance to countless more in the future and live a life that is harmonious and productive without having to sell their soul. She is vocal, and she does not shy away from explaining things as they are, because she firmly believes that sugar-coating anything, or trying to dodge the point, only causes more confusion. She explains things the way they are, and that is what allows her to instill a sense of right and wrong in these younger minds.

"When you go with your heart, you can't go wrong."

Jen's Parents

Deep-Rooted Integrity

People with strong, deep-rooted integrity, are usually well aware of what is going on around them. They can easily decipher the message, crack the code and look at the bigger picture that these predators are trying to cover up. This also allows them to be able to make more moral and ethical decisions. They can dodge these attempts of luring them into something a lot darker and sinister. However, not all are equipped with such deep-rooted integrity.

Jen wrote a mission statement 13 years ago, and today, that motto is recited every day, especially by girls who are newcomers. Her 39 girls who are in this group have memorized Jen's phone number by heart, and she has assured them that they can call her any time of the day, and she will be there to attend their calls. Whenever they have their meals, they stand up, place a hand on their heart, and recite their motto and prayers. The process of doing this over and over again helps girls feel empowered, proud and confident. For 13 years, this has been the case, and this exercise continues to provide a source of strength, confidence and courage for years to come.

Jen relates by telling her life story and what she had to endure. When she was 14, her mother developed a debilitating disease.

This meant that her mother wasn't the breadwinner of the house anymore and things quickly became rough. Jen had to work through three jobs a day, and she never shared this with anyone at the time. She would go through multiple shifts, take showers at the local YWCA, and she would put on her suit to work the next job. It was through hard work, dedication and commitment that went on to strengthen her character and integrity. Both of her parents are caregivers. She went through all of these trials and challenges and kept her sheer integrity at the forefront. Her story and her life-long struggles serve as a benchmark and as an inspiration for these girls, hence allowing them to learn directly from Jen how to better lead their lives.

She is especially able to relate to teenagers who are going through an identity crisis. There was a time where she was also struggling to figure out who she was, and where she came from. Many would call her 'Paki,' a slang word used to discriminate against Pakistani citizens, and she would often find herself getting frustrated and angry. However, it was her parents who taught her how to own the fact that she was different. She does that daily and today, she teaches other teenagers to own their special backgrounds. Through her experience, she has been able to empower them, allow them to feel special and gives them permission to be different as well. By developing deep-rooted integrity, she does what many others would easily fail at; empowering the youth.

For someone as tough and as dedicated as Jen, one would imagine it would be impossible for her to be struck by depression or frustration, however, Jen recalls how bullying went on to affect her. She would be called names, would be left out of sports, and kids made fun of her, all of that left permanent mental scars. Reflecting on those memories still brings tears to the surface. She admits that had an opportunity to join gangs, do drugs or drink alcohol presented itself, she might have gone for them. Fortunately, that did not happen, and by the time she landed in Toronto, she had already developed deep-rooted integrity that allowed her to steer clear of drugs, gangs, violence and crimes.

At the age of 31, she went on to become a police officer. Before she did that, she worked in different regions, including far away in Florida She worked in a law firm, was an event coordinator, and also worked on a TV show called "Single-Girl Diaries." She wanted to explore the world and find out what it had to offer.

Growing up, travel was just not possible given their financial situation. By this time, Jen's mother was no longer able to walk. When her mom knew about all these possible ventures, she encouraged Jen to go for it. She of course, and said y yes to these opportunities, allowing to travel the world but also to learn more about life outside her bubble.

During this time, she felt a need to do something that helped others. She wanted to serve others, and in a specific city where she could make a difference. She wanted to help people, and she wanted to start a charity. While she was in the force, it was her ultimate goal to start her philanthropy journey and truly make a difference that mattered. Policing went on to serve as a much-needed bridge to connect her to her dreams, she is so thankful. She is proud to have chosen the police line of work because it is through that, that she was able to set up a foundation and help make a difference the way she does now.

Jen continues to serve her community both as a mentor other kids and is a decorated police officer. She has saved a significant number of lives and is poised to do a lot more for the world. She has a lot more to give, and more to teach. To her this is just a start!

Girlz Will Be Girlz

The name of the foundation that Jen established for her girls comes from wanting power to come from within While she isn't allowed to put on much makeup as a police officer or leave her hair untied, she is still a girl from within. When the time came to choose a name for the foundation, she was true to her nature, hence the name.

The foundation has gone on to provide support and shelter to many children, up to the age of 25. Despite her incredibly demanding job as a detective, which received a promotion recently, she always finds the time to hang out with the ones she mentors. She is a true source of inspiration, comfort and love for these children, while continuing to be their mentor through life, guiding them through their decisions, and standing with them as support. She has chosen to prioritize her foundation over anything else.

What her mother taught her is the foundation and what it means to embodies it. She applies all that she has been taught and ensures that these young women get to witness and experience the same. Through teaching integrity, and guiding them on how to strengthen it, she can help create a difference that is catching a lot of attention from the media in Canada and other news outlets as well. She is becoming a leader of a completely different class, and she deserves all the credit for what she does. Changing one life alone is a huge feat; she has done it 39 times already.

Toni Vanschoyck

Toni has been working with start up network marketing companies for over 20 years after owning 2 successful traditional businesses in landscaping and day care that she started after being burnt out from her corporate restauranteur job. Her track record for success in network marketing in the field and corporate, allowed her to reach top in organizational sales and income.

Currently the team Toni has helped to build over 2 Billon dollars in organizational sales in just over 6 years. She is also the first to earn over one million dollars and be a part of the exclusive MDC (Million dollar club) and has 4 streams of income which brings in multiple 8 figures. She has now earned millions with her network marketing business.

Toni has also sat on advisory boards and has also been a liaison and helped small startups and small business owners through using social media, increasing sales goals, relationship building and retention of current customers and representatives. Toni has proven systems for individuals looking to improve human relationship skills both in the workplace and the home.

Toni has learned a great deal about the industry and being able to do only what a few can do. Teaching and coaching teams of people and individuals has been one of her greatest accomplishments and helping them achieve success. This also helped her to learn how to help others and how to build a brand name.

Toni has also written three best selling Amazon books under the series Effing Simple.

Toni is always working on personal, professional growth and wealth skills.

Her goal is to help leadership in companies and sales initiatives help others to do the same.

Toni has been professionally speaking for over 10 years and has a variety of topics including motivation and success principles and has authored many articles.

Toni's belief in giving back and working with non profits have been a top priority such as Center For Women, the National Heart Association and Habitat For Humanity and now our own non-profit Low Country Love.

Chapter 9

Why

By Toni Vanschoyck

For anyone aspiring to be a leader, or for one who is trying to become a better leader than they already are, you must have a strong why as the author of this book and the two I have previously written the why is always something we touch upon. Why? It is simply because if you do not have a strong 'why' you are never able to envision the road that is presenting itself. Your 'why' from a leadership perspective, should and must be revisited constantly.

It is only natural that with time, you grow, and when you grow your 'why' evolves and changes. Sticking to your initial reasons may quickly become outdated and obsolete. It is why I insist on reviewing and revisiting your whys at least every 6 months. I am not rambling here just because I read this somewhere in a book, or because I think that this is the right thing to do; I know it is! How can you expect to achieve a single thing when you don't know the reason down to your core?

I am what you would call a 'Serial Preneur.' I have recently and successfully launched my fifth business, and that means that I have gathered substantial experience over the years, and have picked up a tremendous amount of knowledge that I have continuously applied throughout my life and career. It is through that experience that I say this with confidence; review your 'why' to move forward.

Figuring Out Your 'Why'

When I started with my first business, it failed and my second one failed. I had already been divorced twice- ya feel me here? I had an abusive parent, abusive user friends, abusive husbands. I was the definition of a fucking shit show and I let people know this every damn day. But I clawed my way out of those personal and professional failures (to many to count).
I was ego driven and basically a huge asshole. I entered into my 40's with such a huge chip on my shoulders.

It was then I finally figured it out. I paid my dues in my past and I launched an amazing business and we took it to the top. We didn't just stop with that. We bought our dream home, had nice cars, discovered a family now (friends are family you can choose), and live my life by design. Before I knew it shortly after, my life stalled. For two years, I was unable to figure out what happened. That's where it hit me; I hadn't taken the time to review my 'why.' I had to get unstuck by realizing that I definitely hadn't achieved it all even though I thought I had.

I had an undiscovered goal that most do. However, what I did not have was the answer to a simple question, "what's next?" I had no idea what I would do once I had achieved my goals. I felt empty and my business took a toll as well. I had achieved what I wanted, but how could I take that to the next level? That is where I reviewed and refined my 'why.'

My leadership 'why' comes from a place of service. You can read many books and articles to try and figure out what motivates you and inspires you, but if you do not have some kind of a big reason that justifies why you are grinding every day, you are essentially stuck in a plateau that never seems to end. Alleviate this and write it down. What do you want? What moves your heart, your soul, your being? You are the only one that can answer this. Answering this will only serve you.

Throughout our lives we have been led to believe that life is waking up, going to work, putting in the 40 hours a week, coming home, have a beer, watch TV for the next few hours before hitting the bed. It is an endless, monotonous cycle that has managed to linger on... Society embraces it! Are you honestly ready to believe this is what life is all about? If so, for what? Pittance? I refuse to believe that, and I reject such a lifestyle every single day of my life. I'm unemployable. I'm serious. I will never let some other fucker get rich off of me.

If that is the end goal of a person, they simply do not have a solid 'why' in their lives. This is the reason why the contributors you have read about have jobs, and yet, they have a grand reason why they keep showing up every day; to contribute to society.

Ask yourself a few questions. Besides contributing to your own family, which is fairly understandable, what do you do on daily basis to:

1. Make yourself better?
2. Make someone else better?
3. Make your community and the world better?

We as a society have fallen for this because most of us have failed miserably at coming up with the answers to these questions. We are doing any of these things consciously, on a daily basis, simply because this is what we have been programmed to do.

For the better part of our lives, we are told to go to college, just so we can land ourselves a "good" job. That is bullshit, yet g I keep hearing that every day. College is NOT cut out for everyone. Of course, if you want to go on and become a doctor, an engineer, or a technician of some sort, you will need continuous education, and college is the place for that. However, what about those who want to be entrepreneurs? What about those of us that don't dream of debt?? Where do entrepreneurs find the education that will serve them in the long run? Surely, mainstream education isn't teaching any of that. They're not even teaching the basics - To never spend more than what you make. and that leaves these aspiring candidates and entrepreneurs with only one choice – seeking out a mentor.

It is through a mentor that entrepreneurs get to learn and experience what entrepreneurship is all about. These mentors are the people who once stood where many stand today and have made it big time. They will guide you through each step of the way and will provide you with all the tools and knowledge you need to work on. All that remains is for you to get your ass off the couch and act.

Entrepreneurs genuinely want to help people through the application of their expertise. It is their 'why' that allows them to do so. This is exactly why I started a non-profit. This is also why some of the women in this book have done the same. It serves us with no financial gains, but what it can deliver is a sense of accomplishment unlike any other.

Breaking the Silence

While I continued to enjoy the rewards that I was receiving from my first business, I felt something was missing. For the next one to two years, my business was on a flat line. There was virtually no positive movement upwards, and this stressed me out and gave me anxiety. I was missing the next 'why' because I was growing comfortable with what I had, and I wasn't doing much to seek the 'why' out for myself.

It was later that I had the opportunity to attend an event where a woman spoke about domestic violence. That was big effing a-ha moment! For those who may not know, I have gone through the horrors of domestic violence myself, and I reside in a state that is ranked number one for domestic violence, which is why I am educated on the subject.

After listening to that speech, I knew what my next venture would be founded on. I knew right away what I was going to have at the core of the idea. It was there that I discovered my 'why' that I had been looking for the last 2 years.

I was able to establish the non-profit and right after I did that, I had my next 'why' waiting for me. When you find it within you to have a reason, a why, you will always find the energy to ensure you see it to fruition. It is through this process that you come across other ideas, concepts and opportunities that can serve you as the next 'why' in your life. I know that because I had found mine. Lowcountry Love (the name of my organization) is solely focused on helping families and children.

I have recently done something else big - HUGE! I established a training center in my own backyard where people will come in as groups and be part of an amazing Effing Simple Leadership Retreat. I will mentor with the help of a few of my friends and of course my husband and partner in shenanigans, and allow them to learn valuable information and gain the confidence to be leaders in their respective ways. The best part about this is that we all learn from each other because we bring different experiences to the table. This idea has come to fruition, today.

We bring in 10 - 12 people. They're only requirements are to cover their expenses, and in return, they get to hang out with us and be mentored directly with full attention. It not only gives our clients partners a chance to learn from us, but it also paves the way for us to learn from them. A leader never takes their learning hat off.

I didn't figure out my 'why' for a long time, but you can do it a lot faster than me. You don't have to wait to be 45 years old to figure it out. Or, maybe you're reading this and you're in your 50s, 60s, or 70s. You are never too old, too young, too ANYTHING- Just start! Yes, I faced obstacles, one relating to my heart issues that I discovered in 2019, which almost killed me (congenital hole in my heart) I had never been in a hospital, been told that I have to slow down, and those nine months were really monumentally tough on me. The good thing was that I used 9 months to reflect upon myself., This allowed me to put things into perspective, and helped me to move forward as someone better prepared to handle challenges and opportunities in the future.

Helping Others

Sometimes, we find our whys by helping others. Almost a year ago, a dear friend approached me and told me about an incredible product that she had to offer. The challenge was she had no idea how to move ahead. Being a person of faith, knowing that God wanted me to help her out because it was His will to put her in my path. I have known her for five years and she has an incredible work ethic. Just recently, we signed all the papers, and the fact that I was able to do something for a local business owner and friend means a hell of a lot to me. Not only is it something fun, but I genuinely believe the product will go on to be a top product, in its specific niche.

None of this would have been possible had I not searched for the 'why' that had gone missing in my life.

Whatever I was doing, I had to go back and ask myself some simple yet important questions:

1. Why am I doing this?
2. How is it serving me?
3. Does it bring me joy?

If my answer would not be able to justify all three questions, it had to go out of my life. There was no reason why I should carry on doing something that did not bring joy to me, that was not serving me or had no purpose to me. Whatever it had to be it must be able to provide a satisfactory answer. For anyone who feels lost, or is looking for their next 'why,' ask yourself these questions and answer as honestly as possible.

Moving On

Once a person discovers the 'why,' there is always going to be a reason for a person to continue doing what they do best. If something goes wrong, they should come up with another strong reason why they should continue, or what they should start focusing on. Successful people never stop, and part of the reason is that they always look towards the Next. Big. Thing. They are always seeking out how they can take their success to the next level, and as long as there is an answer, they will put in the efforts needed to bring that idea, that 'why' to fruition.

I may have been stuck back then, however, I was still consistent and I showed up to work every day. Leaders with strong whys will do the same thing. No matter what.

"If you do not show up, you no longer have a business."

People do business with you because people trust you over others. As an entrepreneur, a small business owner, or even a service provider, you are doing a service by serving your clients every day. I service those around me, including my team members, business partners, and those that I want to help be successful.

Throughout all of the bullshit that we all went through last year, I made sure that small business owners that I cared about, loved and respected got business from me. I was showing up for them not because I had any personal agendas or motives, but because I wanted them to know that I was there to support them, period. I am proud to say that I did that, and I will continue to do so until I am no longer able to do so until I am dead in my coffin.

Throughout this phase in life, there has been one person that has moved me, and inspired me to do so much: Dave Portnoy. On the off-chance that he gets to read this, I would love to tell him that he is my hero and that I would love to meet him one day. It is because of him that I discovered another big 'why.' I want to be that person, (just like Kid Rock & Sean Whalen and donate selflessly to Portnoy's non-profit), "here's a 100K to help you get your matters sorted." That's my ultimate goal, and that's my 'why' that keeps me going forward.

Dave Portnoy, is a fearless leader. He knows his whys better than any of us can imagine, and he knows what he is supposed to do. Unlike the majority of us, who would often give things a second thought, he believes in what he does and goes for it – end of the story. That's the kind of person I am and will continue to be.

There are things that I am fearless at and areas where I do need to work to be 100% fearless. I am not saying that I can't do it because the fact is that I will spend the rest of my life, trying to do exactly that – become fearless.

While I am doing what I do, I have noticed adults and leaders who tend to drift away from their goals, their reasons for their endless struggles, and it pains me to say that I see them do it every single day. I say adults because when was the last time you saw a child discouraged about something that didn't come to fruition? Never. They keep trying until they get it. Instead of looking for something bigger in life, people tend to settle for the status quo. These are the kind of people who will always convince you that they will go on to do something and that something just never happens. They are liars. Plain and simple.

There are some who will read the above and go "why on earth is Toni hurt if others fail to do something with their lives?" There is a logical reason for that. It is one thing to sympathize, meaning that you just say words to make others feel like you care, and it is a completely different thing to empathize. The latter is where we say things because we have been through such an ordeal ourselves, and I am not an exception to that. At the age of 40, I was filing for bankruptcy. It wasn't because I had a bad business plan, but it was because I didn't have my shit together. I was unable to focus on things that mattered and I apocalyptically failed at finance. I didn't have a good relationship or understanding of money. I had no solid why and I didn't have a vision beyond what I had already accomplished. I didn't have anyone else to blame for that except me.

Failure that I experienced almost seven years ago, however, is what taught me lessons that are the most valuable to me. Today, I still am the same person, but a lot smarter, wiser and far more motivated than I was ever before. It is simply because of the failure I experienced taught me really valuable lessons, and I was eager and willing to learn them and not repeat mistakes.

Chapter 10

Finance

By Toni Vanschoyck

The first thing that I notice is the reason that people are trying to get out of whatever they may currently be doing - it's essential because of the money factor. For them it's a quick and easy fix, but the real problem lies in the fact that they don't have a money mindset. This is the root cause of all financial challenges.

Yes, they go on to join network marketing or something else because they present themselves as money-making machines, but only a rare few make the kind of money they are hoping for. The problem lies within our society and what 95% of us are taught from childhood. t. We all have been raised with mediocrity and the scarcity mindset of never having enough.

TONI VANSCHOYCK

My dad hails from a blue-collar family, and he did fairly well throughout his life and career. My dad wasn't the kind of dad that most would think, and that naturally left me with the wrong kind of money mindset. Whatever I learned, I did so through experience and my willingness to do so.

Ever since I was 15, I started working extremely hard. I was limited to work only through the weekends, and that meant I would get home at 1 AM on Saturday. The very same day, I would then go to work at 8 AM, and work to my bones till 1 AM once again. The following morning, I would do the same until I knew my 40-hour work week target was met. As soon as I turned 18, I was kicked out, but that did not stop me from doing all the hard work I did and pouring in the relentless efforts.

Today, I do what I love, and that is I because I had to get into the zone and the right mindset to do so. It took years for me to figure quite a few things out, but that doesn't mean that it should take anyone the same amount of time to do the things I can do today. I teach others what I have learned through experience, mistakes & wins, and I hope that my knowledge and insights will set things straight for many, allowing them an easier passage into a successful life when applied

The Fault in Our Society

One of the main things I stress is that no one should buy something they can't afford. Being debt-free is the new sexy, and I agree with that statement 100%. If you want to buy something that you cannot afford, don't fucking buy it! t, Strap down and put in the effort, and prove that you are worthy of it by earning a sizable income, save your money and then buy it yourself. Pay cash, screw the credit cards.

Debt is a shackle. Money is just a medium of exchange, but the way we have been brought up, it is far more than that. Here's a simple rule to follow: If you think money will do good, it will do good, and if you think it will do bad, it will do bad! There is no middle ground, and there is no grey area for anyone to explore.

We have been led to believe that if we want to get into a college, we have to arrange for a student loan, and that life will be good. This is just another load of bullshit that many of us still believe to be true. Life will be anything but good. It will come back and haunt us for the rest of our lives. It is a system that has been designed to ensure that we never get to truly live for ourselves. Dependency. All of us should want to be the furthest distance from dependency as possible. By taking a loan today, we are essentially handing over our lives, our finances and our earnings to clowns who sit behind their spacious office desk and push some numbers here and there so that they can go spend quality time with their families on a private island, while the rest of us work for life, just to repay a loan that is dangling over us like a bird diving down for prey. They know that there is money to be made by crippling Americans.

    Whether you become a neurosurgeon, a day trader, or even something bigger, if you are not able to afford it, don't do it. Your parents or your children are not liable for your actions or your future career path, you are. Do not hurl the burden on their shoulders because they have already been through some challenges in life, just so you can get a decent education. I know many young adults will be reading this, and to them I say, I had to make my way. Yes, my dad paid for my education, but I took care of all my living expenses on my own. It was a mutual relationship that I carried forward. Life can be quite challenging, especially if you are living on your own, are a single parent and trying to go to school. Despite all that, I never made any excuses, and I went on to finish what I started. Finish what you start. Period.

    I want my children to find their path, but before they can go on to do that, I need to teach them how to balance their bank accounts. I do so by teaching them how to write down everything that they are spending and everything that they are bringing in. I emphasize the importance of having a positive or excess amount that ends on the side of the book every month. That, to me, is the first step towards gaining the

FINANCE

right financial mindset. Without it, we cannot even imagine going anywhere forward.

Moving on, it is important to understand that this isn't a comparison game. Just because all of your friends are going to college does not mean that you have to do the same. Every single child of mine ended up getting a job in the restaurant industry. Why? The food and beverage industry goes on to teach you how to develop your patience, social and appreciation skills, and it does so unlike any other. Yes, it is tedious and cumbersome, but that is just part of the learning curve. It is the humblest of industries to work in, and it allows you to groom yourself through hard work and patience into a completely new, confident and prepared person.

Naomi, my daughter, worked in the restaurant industry for two years, and that is where she honed her skills. Whenever I came in, her co-workers always boasted about her work ethic. She went on to become our assistant, because she had already had great people skills. She helped us with our first business and has an entrepreneurial mindset. She gets raises and bonuses based on her performance, and the business she creates for us. I will point out that she has yet to attend college. I encouraged her to take a couple of business classes, but I see massive success for her already.

If you are aiming to become a great leader in life, it is imperative that you understand and grasp the concept of money, how it can either ruin you or create great success.

However, money is only one of the 5 Pillars of Life. You may have already figured out the 'why' in your life, but this is where you must figure out the 'how' and remain true to your principles. Never go on to spend a dime on things that you cannot afford or need in life. Ditch the Starbucks and stop going out twice a week, then figure out your finances. It will blow your mind! Do the hard work first and become the kind of leader that is chased by money, not the other way around.

Money Matters

For most of us, it is those little purchases that we make every day that matter the most. We go on to do things like buying a $5 cup of coffee or settling with an $8 dinner., but once you start adding the numbers up, it becomes pretty obvious that it is anything but feasible. Buy what you need and prepare meals at home for 50% of the cost. It saves you a shit ton of money, and it is a lot healthier as well.

Once again, it is our crippling society that is to be blamed because we have been groomed in a culture where it is "normal," to stop by the nearest coffee shop and buy a cup of designer coffee that you may not even consume completely, and throw most of it away. Then, there are the countless deli stops that we make or the famous chicken shop around the corner that sells incredible kung pao takeaways. If that wasn't enough, we then go on to make little purchases

FINANCE

online, and we end up buying a lot more than what we need. In addition, social media is stepping in, with pop up advertisements of cute boutique shops, new gadgets, Amazon finds...etc. that you can lay your hands on. These are all impulse purchases, and they can negatively affect anyone's financial standing in a matter of seconds.

The irony is that we do this every month, and by the end of the month, we are always trying to tell ourselves never to do that again, and guess what? That is the same story that plays out the next month and the next, and so on. This has got to stop. Every time we spend something, we should do so only if it is necessary, only if it is genuinely something we need. Otherwise, those two $5 cups of coffee each (I make way better coffee anyway as can you), the $10 meal that we buy, if we add those numbers up, we end up spending $600 a month for things that could have cost us $150, had we bought the items ourselves and made a meal or two at home. Let's not even throw Target into the conversation...This has got to stop!

Yes, it does take some getting used to but that is a major part of learning. Through such changes, you will come to realize just how much you end up saving by the end of the month and eventually the year.

Multiplying Money

Money attracts money, and that's the rule that has existed ever since. Our first business gave us the ability to establish our Effing Simple platform. That was money well-earned because it allowed us to generate more money. The profits we gathered from that, we went on to put it into the next business idea, and that gave us yet another income source. Guess what? That was further invested we ended up with three sources. None of this would have been possible had I thought to spend all that hard-earned money on fancy dinners, luxury items, exotic vacations. Have we done that? Yes, we have, but we put the time, effort and work in to be at this point. I love to invest. I keep an eye out for a good investment opportunity, and I invest my money accordingly. This helps generate additional income on top of the other streams that I have already mentioned. It helps us generate a profit, and I tell others if they want to be entrepreneurs, they have to hire their own professionals. They have to find a good business lawyer, CPA, and accountant, and none of this is negotiable. It is through hiring these experts that you get to learn more about your business and how to best monetize it.

    A great CPA needs to be is amazing, and he/ she has to serve in helping save a massive chunk of money through expertise. However, just because they have expertise does not mean you should remain quiet. Once you hire a firm, have

FINANCE

them track your activities for 30 days, and then assess your situation. When you find a good CPA to look where the gaps are, you will end up with solutions. These solutions will be what's best for you. At the end of the day, everything can be written off when you're a small business.

These little expenditures, add up to something massive at the end of the month. When we spot them and avoid them, we can save ourselves some serious cash, hence eliminating the need to ever fall for the idea of 'borrowing' money from banks, or using those evil credit cards that will eventually devour you into a vicious, never-ending cycle of repayments.

All the big box stores, massive shopping outlets are designed by incredibly genius people, to get you to spend money and often times money you don't have. They use specialized psychological tactics, by strategically placing adverts and products so that you, will walk in thinking "I'm only going to buy myself one item," but then you walk out with 9 other items that you did not initially have on your mind. Knowing that you could only spend so much, you still go past your budget. They make you think you need it.

I am trying to point out that impulse purchases are a threat and we should all learn to identify and eliminate. It is only natural that you may be saving up to buy yourself a dream home, or a vehicle that you intend to buy by the end of this year, and that's dandy. If you have the cash, go ahead, but don't put yourself in a box However, don't allow yourself to buy things that just popped up on your screen. Delayed gratification has huge power. Budget, budget, budget.

You should always know where your money is going, what you are purchasing, how much you have left, every single day. There is no shortcut to this exercise Whether you keep a ledger, a simple money diary, or maintain a spreadsheet, record your cash flow. You may be the finest doctor, the best lawyer, or even a renowned engineer, but you can never be truly free and successful, or go on to become an entrepreneur, until you develop this habit of knowing what's coming in and what's going out. This is what helps you get into the zone of a money mindset that you will need to excel in life.

I get it if you are someone who isn't good with numbers, I wasn't. Still ain't. However, just because we may not be the brightest bulb, it doesn't mean we can't keep track of the obvious. If you are unable to maintain a record of your finances, find someone qualified enough to get the job done or is able. You must manage your own money that you have worked so hard for or find someone trustworthy and qualified who can do the numbers for you, and don't let them move a cent without your approval.

People have stopped valuing money and have started an endless shopping spree that is stacking up their credit card debt. I genuinely believe that if you have credit card debt, you are a slave to the man. It goes to show just how easily you

FINANCE

can mismanage your finances, and not value what you have earned after years of struggle.

When it comes to finances, leadership is more than just a tool of exchange. For anyone to be a successful leader, they must become a <u>champion of their finances.</u> That is the first and foremost thing. When you get to a level of success, you then have the option to hire others to do what you don't want to do. Consider this as an investment into yourself to know what your finances are. There is not a possible way where you can invest in yourself without controlling and knowing what you're spending habits look like. You have so many applications and softwares out there that can help you learn more about your financial behavior. You can apply to one right now and enter every single purchase. I strive for you to take notice and stop the bleeding dollars. I give you permission to stop and create your network.

Finally, there is the point of having that incredible peace of mind, and the ability to go to bed and sleep easily, and that all comes once you know what your financial position is.   When we were filing for bankruptcy, things were quite bleak. My husband and considered splitting up. There is no denying that finances are one of the top reasons why couple choose to split. Once things started to get back on the right track, we experienced an improvement in all directions. We are able to have open communication about finances. We no longer have debt, and things have never been better., It was our money mindset that was at the core of our challenges and it is the very same that has allowed us to bond together better than ever before.

"Money is like oxygen. You need it to breathe."

Rita Davenport

Chapter 11

Mind and Vision

By Toni Vanschoyck

Mindset leads to vision. Vision leads to mindset. It's a synergistic relationship. If you are someone who has a negative and messy mindset, or one that is not organized, you will never be able to figure out what your life is going to be like after a few months, years or decades.

Leaders are visionaries. However, while they may be visionary, they are also able to see far ahead in time. When a leader has challenges, such as facing naysayers, they must always retain a positive mindset, even if it is uncomfortable. These leaders must then address the issues, find the relevant solutions to the problems, and be able to visualize and paint the picture of what the results will look like.

Many business owners usually deal with situations and scenarios as they come, with the exception of leaders. You must be proactive vs. reactive. The leaders differ because of their ability to foresee matters and plan well ahead. They can anticipate something coming their way, and when it comes, they are already miles ahead. While the rest of the team may struggle to come up with a viable solution, the leader would simply walk in and present the solution. This is through experience. It's learned.

The Right Mindset

Every business, regardless of how profitable it may be, has highs and lows. There is no escaping either of these, and both of these go on to test leaders When the chips are down, a true leader will rise and present solutions. They are solution driven. Every entrepreneur knows there is an ebb and flow to business. It is understood that if a company is not doing its best, everyone is tested. This is where a true leader shines bright and goes on to become that iconic hero, and seems to save the company almost single-handedly, when that isn't the case.

Now, you might imagine that if the business is already on the top, leaders can kick back and relax. It is now that these leaders must up their game and face an even bigger challenge; how to make things even better? You have to create more value.

A business is not a short-term project. A job on the other hand is. When you start a business, you're putting your heart and soul into it for as long as you can We don't half ass it. When you get a job, you may think you will serve for as long as possible, but a year or two down the road you will be willing to take the next opportunity and jump ship. It is human nature and happens every day. Your business, on the other hand, will go on to remain for decades to come.

As long as you know what your passion is and are committed to what you are doing, plus have a solid vision for the future of your business, it will prosper. Take that away and you are going to be trading time for money. How can you tell if you are doing the latter? If you are waiting for the doors to open, just so you can make some money, you are not in a visionary state of mind, and your vision will be limited to the financial gains only. That is not an entrepreneurial leadership vision.

While you may work on your vision, it is important to know and remember that nothing in life is to be taken for granted, and you cannot go on to 'wait' for opportunities to come by. You may expect a few doors to open for you, through which you will be able to earn a certain amount of income, but there is no guarantee. 2020 alone caused so many problems and panic for everyone in the world. Nobody predicted such a catastrophe, and most were left to pull their hair out, worrying about the losses they were suffering when our great country was founded on small businesses.

Aim for More

Here is a general rule of thumb; any additional source of income is effectively an insurance policy, but make the main thing the main thing. As an entrepreneur, it's so important to have these multiple sources of income because if one of the doors were to close tomorrow, it wouldn't leave you with anxiety and the, "What now?!". You will always have additional income streams to support you, and help you to move forward. Having multiple sources of income, therefore, is yet another non-negotiable.

This is why I recommend other entrepreneurs to have something consumable, that has e-commerce options it's are no longer optional; online business has become a necessity

As an entrepreneur, you must constantly look for new opportunities that you can generate revenue from. Never settle for just one, thinking that things are good as they are because if the last year has taught us anything, it is to ensure we have multiple sources of income.

"Leadership is learned; you're not born with it."

MIND AND VISION

People often called me bossy from a very young age. I was a leader in the making, and I certainly was able to delegate matters. I would assign tasks to team members based on what they were good at. As leaders, it is up to us to highlight the strengths and weaknesses and help others find out how they can hone in on strengths and outsource weaknesses. As John Maxwell puts it:

"You never wanna be a 5-pin in a category, and try to make yourself a 7. You go take those 8s or 9s, and you go make yourself 10."

You have to surround yourself with people who are better than you. For anyone to be a professional, one needs to go through thousands of hours before they are anywhere near being one, and that is a lot of time. Leadership happens every single day.

Since leadership is a daily job, reading something provides a daily dose of growing skills. Major entrepreneurs and CEOs go on to read 50 plus books in a year. These are books that are packed with values, lessons, tips and suggestions, none of which they knew before. They learned through trial and error like I have. It is through these books, failures and curveballs, that visionary leaders continue to learn something new every single day.

To sum up, it is vital for you, or any entrepreneur in the making to:

- Know what you are good at and focus on these qualities.
- Emphasize the strengths, and make them better
- Outsource your weaknesses
- Always something new and get great at it.
- Have multiple income streams
- Never settle.
- Never stop dreaming.

Prioritize Your Strengths

It makes perfect sense, right? Why spend 100 hours on something you are terrible at when you can hire someone to do the same job in an hour, saving you 100 hours to do something productive instead? That, right there, is what entrepreneurs are all about; working on their strengths while outsourcing the weakness.

I know, a lot of people would think why should they go on to outsource anything, but let me tell you this; you cannot go on to create a vision if you are far too caught up doing everything on your own. You have to learn how to let go of things that you can't handle and outsource them. By doing so, you end up creating extra time for yourself, allowing you to not only do what you do best but create a vision for your endeavors and plan accordingly.

I have seen mothers who are handling their children, cleaning up their houses, and still expecting to keep the entrepreneur within them alive. Is it possible? No, because something always falls short. Responsibilities are never-ending, and that automatically means that they should either outsource for the cleaning and handling the household chores. The first thing I teach is to hire a housecleaner. Those hours can be spent on the income producing activities and letting someone else clean better. It's no longer a one woman/man show.

I have always ensured that my children know how to pull their weight. I wanted them to learn how to value their own time and those around them. It has worked, and I can see positive results coming from all directions.

The Rewarding Contributions

I gave my children money, as a reward, to read productive books (emphasis on productive) when they had free time. During their school weeks, they were simply not allowed to watch any TV, use phones, or any other form of entertainment. Even on the weekends, I placed a strict reward system where they were allowed to watch TV only if they had done all their chores.

TONI VANSCHOYCK

The reward system helped me to help my children learn so much about life, the challenges it brings and prepared them to handle these situations as they come. I tasked each of my children to choose a chore and it was their weekly responsibility Sometimes, one would do the laundry while the other cleaned the house, cooked, or mowed the lawn. It wasn't because I didn't want to do it, but purely because I wanted them to be prepared for the future. There will eventually come a time where all of my children will have to get up and walk into the professional world, all on their own. By being able to do all of these chores, they know how to manage their own lives effectively. While others would say I was rude or harsh, the fact is that these habits, if encouraged from a very young age, will help our kids excel in a lot of areas for their future life. There is only so much a parent can do for children. They can only hold their hand and walk them for a while before a time comes when the child must let go and walk his way.

I wanted to ensure that I raise independent adults, and I don't regret any of the things that I have done in life for them. I have taught them lessons, the worth of which they will realize eventually. Don't get me wrong, I am super proud of my children, and how they continue to contribute to their current responsibilities. They are stepping up, taking initiative and carrying out the right actions.

MIND AND VISION

The Power of Positivity

There is no denying that we as human beings will have to face the negativity within us - it's our nature. Negativity is based on fear of the unknown. The "what ifs?" It takes practice and patience to see the positive when you feel you're in a losing battle or something isn't going right. Positivity is more powerful than I can go on to define in words. How do I do it? Let me explain.

Many people seek and search for answers elsewhere, without realizing that the answers are inside of them. Through positive practices, especially the ones that promote productivity and tolerance can help you tackle difficult situations easily. It is through positivity that a true pacesetter emerges, and it is through the same positivity that they conquer their challenges. A simple exercise is to write down everything that is going right; business or life. Take that negative thought and write down the positive one opposite of it.

Positive practices; you already know a lot of them. These include activities reading personal development books, listening to podcasts (people that have actually made it), improving your people skills, all of these are positive activities. These are a few practices that will you use your strengths. You have to be responsible for what goes in and what goes out, and you must be willing to teach yourself the lessons that you need in life. When it comes to finances, you must adopt positivity and focus on the good while discarding the bad.

Guarding the Positive Mindset

For me, TV and the news are no longer my sources of information or temporary satisfaction. There is far too much negativity that is being showcased every day and it's a waste of my time and a needless evil that I simply cannot afford to have in life. As entrepreneur, I have to believe that there is humanity that prevails, and that means keeping a positive mindset. If we allow the trash-talking news channels to fill our minds with their negativity, we will end up losing sight of our vision, and struggle to find reasons to move forward in life. Most of the information on television is biased anyway. The only knowledge that comes to help is the one you have read about, experienced and seen for yourself.

I do everything to protect my positive mindset. I get up every morning and I do a gratitude exercise. I remind myself what I am grateful for before I do anything else. It only takes 5 minutes, but it is relieving and powerful. To me, that is non-negotiable, even if I wake up late.

Next, I go through my morning routine, and that is where I do my personal development, exercise, and focus on what's on my mind. I don't let anyone distract me before the stroke of the noon. I take care of all my appointments and business matters. The evening is where I handle calls and other business-related tasks. That's how scheduled and organized my life is, and that is just how I like it. What about you? What are your non-negotiables?

To many, waking up bright and early and then giving that time to their work may be the way forward I have a mentality that the morning time is mine, and mine alone. I cannot do anything for anyone before I do things for myself, and that's what my mornings are all about. This may not work for everyone, and such is the case with Naomi, my daughter, because she prefers working in the morning and her time is in the late afternoon/evening.

Every entrepreneur needs to respect, guard and maintain their positive mindset., They can resonate at a completely different frequency, allowing them to attract the kind of results they get. If they remain positive, God showers them with positive. If it is negativity a person is living in they will forever live a life of mediocrity.

Being a leader is all about love; loving people and loving yourself! You must learn how to love everything and everyone in life, and above all, you must learn how to love the process even when you hit the rough patches. Consider this as the ultimate key to your entire entrepreneurial experience. I don't know who you are, where you are from, and I don't even know in what ways if this helps you, but know that as an entrepreneur, I love and respect who you are. We are all in this to make this world a better place for others. We are the ones who have worked so much that losing is simply not an option. We either create a history or we go rewrite it.

    This book is not meant to be "just another in the series," but it is purely because I wanted to share with the world just how much IMPACT we leading entrepreneurs and contributors can make on the world. By meeting these great people, I have learned from about compassion, love, positivity, gratitude, faith and leading with my heart, all of that has helped me become a better person. I met them through a journey that began a couple of years ago and had I not decided to change my life, I would have never come to know of these great souls. The impact that they have had on my life is just phenomenal, and I can only imagine just how much impact we have the power to make on the rest of the world. Throughout this journey, I have met many, many people, mentors and more, each of which has gone on to teach me something truly incredible. To them, I say "Thank you!"

Conclusion

Leadership isn't something we are born with; it is something we pick up on and learn. *Effing Simple Leadership* may be the third book in the series, but this one was special. I have met some of the most incredible people on the planet, and that was only because they and I went on to pursue common goals; to make a better world, to contribute to the lives of people, and to be great leaders one day.

Each one of the contributors, who graciously found the time to go through this project with me, have gone on to experience hardships the likes of which most of us can only fathom. They have gone through the thick and the thin and still managed to come out the other side victorious. They have proven to the world that leadership isn't about being rude or bullying others, forcing them to do what you want them to do, but it is all about love, gratitude and affect through which others are inspired. I hope that you are inspired as much as I am. Love y'all! (you know I am blowing you kisses).

At the heart of it all, none of us, myself included, have anything to gain. Yes, we may be operating our businesses, but the true benefactors are the people who have been through the same things as we have. We may not know who they are, but we certainly know and feel what they have had to endure. My constant goal in life has been to be that person who would always stand in support of the oppressed, become their voice, and let them know "I'm there for you!"

The world may be a populated place, but kindness, affection and compassion are missing in a lot of areas of business. We could have chosen to mind our own business, but that is just not us. We do not let our weaknesses or inability to act define us; no! As leaders, as entrepreneurs, we make the tough choices, we set the rules, and above all, we tell the world what is right and what isn't

I have been blessed to have so much success, joy and happiness in life, and it is my goal to spread that and share all of that with people who have been deprived of these or need more of. Some goals are far more rewarding than money could give, and this is exactly what it means to me. By teaching others all about leadership, how to manage their finances, and have positivity, I intend to help young entrepreneurs know what leadership is all about, and how they can go on to become one themselves.

I certainly do hope that our stories were able to inspire someone, somewhere in the world. We too were once driven by inspirational people and stories that continue to lead us even today. Our geographical location, race, color or language does not differentiate us; it is our ability to lead or follow that truly defines the kind of people we are. With that said, I bid you farewell, and hope that one day, someone will approach me in the future, telling me how they were moved by one of the stories of this book. That, right there, would be our reward!

Made in the USA
Monee, IL
19 May 2021